Mid-Maryland

Mid-Maryland

A Crossroads of History

Volume One

Michael A. Powell and Bruce A. Thompson, Editors

Published by The History Press
18 Percy Street
Charleston, SC 29403
866.223.5778
www.historypress.net

Copyright © 2005 by Michael A Powell and Bruce A. Thompson
All rights reserved

Cover image: Thomas Cowperthwaite, "New Map of Maryland and Delaware, with their Canals, Roads & Distances [Baltimore inset], 1850." *Courtesy of the Maryland State Archives, Special Collections (Huntingfield Map Collection) MSA SC 1399-1-15.*

First published 2005

Manufactured in the United Kingdom

ISBN 1.59629.071.4

Library of Congress Cataloging-in-Publication Data

Mid-Maryland : a crossroads of history / edited by Michael A. Powell and Bruce A. Thompson.
　　p. cm.
　Selected historical papers from three conferences hosted by the Catoctin Center for Regional Studies along with the National Park Service and Frederick Community College: the Millennium Crossroads conference, held Sept. 29-30, 2000; Crossroads in History: New Perspectives on the Catoctin Region, held in 2002; and Catoctin Crossroads: Folk Traditions and History in Mid-Maryland, held in 2004.
　Includes index.
　ISBN 1-59629-071-4 (alk. paper)
　1. Catoctin Mountain Region (Md.)--History--Congresses. 2. Frederick County (Md.)--History--Congresses. 3. Frederick Region (Md.)--History--Congresses. I. Powell, Michael A. II. Thompson, Bruce A., 1962-
　F187.F8M53 2005
　975.2'87--dc22
　　　　　　　　　　　2005023979

Notice: The information in this book is true and complete to the best of our knowledge. It is offered without guarantee on the part of the author or The History Press. The editors and The History Press disclaim all liability in connection with the use of this book.

All rights reserved. No part of this book may be reproduced or transmitted in any form whatsoever without prior written permission from the publisher except in the case of brief quotations embodied in critical articles and reviews.

To our parents for their love and support:

Albert M. Powell Jr. and Louellen V. Powell
Lowell L. Thompson and Janice G. Roush

Contents

Acknowledgements	9
Introduction	13

African American History — 15

"I Went Down to the Crossroads": — 17
    Runaway Slave Strategies of Colonial and
    Early Federal-era Maryland African Americans
Cheryl Fox

From Slave to Abolitionist: — 29
    James W.C. Pennington of Washington County, Maryland
Dean Herrin

Segregated Salaries: — 39
    The Struggle to Equalize Teachers' Salaries in Frederick County
Bruce A. Thompson

Civil War Era — 51

Thoreau and His American Hero: — 55
    In Support of John Brown's "Raid"
Jessica A. Cannon

"With Her Southern Sisters": 67
    Frederick County and the Election of 1860
Michael A. Powell

Frederick's Confederate Son: 81
    Bradley Tyler Johnson, Brigadier General, C.S.A.
Brian S. Baracz

War on the Homefront: 95
    Sharpsburg Residents during the Battle of Antietam
Edith Wallace

Frederick's Citizens: 111
    Caring for the Civil War Sick and Wounded
Kari Turner

HISTORIC MEMORY AND PRESERVATION 121

Cultural Resources Management: 123
    A Delicate Balance—The Campbell Farmstead
Katherine Grandine

Frederick's French Connection at *L'Hermitage* on the Monocacy Battlefield: 135
    Victoire Vincendiere and French Planter Refugees
    from the Slave Revolt in Haiti in the 1790s
Paula Stoner Reed

The Colonel Thomas Cresap Standing Stone Project 145
Francis Zumbrun

Threatened Treasures: 153
    Creating Endangered Lists
Mary McCarthy

CONTRIBUTORS 169
NOTES 173
INDEX 187

Acknowledgements

The Catoctin Center for Regional Studies, along with the National Park Service and Frederick Community College, has hosted three conferences within the past five years. The first, the "Millennium Crossroads" conference, was held on September 29–30, 2000, and was a huge success, with over two hundred people attending each day of the two-day conference. Two other equally successful conferences followed: "Crossroads in History: New Perspectives on the Catoctin Region" (2002) and "Catoctin Crossroads: Folk Traditions and History in Mid-Maryland" (2004). Culling through the presentations, Doctors Powell and Thompson have selected the best of the papers presented. The first of two projected volumes, this work is a compilation of select papers from the "Millennium Crossroads" conference.

Conferences and publishing projects do not just happen. There are a multitude of people that make such efforts possible. At the start of the "Millennium Crossroads" conference, Frederick Community College (FCC) President Dr. Patricia Stanley, National Park Service Director Robert Stanton, United States Senator Paul Sarbanes and C&O Canal National Historic Park Superintendent Doug Faris welcomed the conferees. Workshops on historic preservation initiatives within Mid-Maryland and at the Chesapeake & Ohio (C&O) Canal followed, with afternoon sessions devoted to current historical research in the Mid-Maryland area. The first day concluded with a tour of the C&O Canal. Sixteen sessions covering African American history, the Civil War, historical preservation and other research topics highlighted the second day.

Mid-Maryland: A Crossroads of History

The "Millennium Crossroads" conference was a model of collaboration, which was the key to the conference's success. The members of the steering committee—representing the historical societies of Carroll, Frederick and Washington Counties, Frederick County Historic Sites Consortium, Frederick City Planning Office and the National Park Service sites in the region—bought into the idea of a regional conference. They helped with the planning and publicizing of the conference. The steering committee members were: Bruce Thompson, FCC coordinator, Catoctin Center for Regional Studies; Dean Herrin, National Park Service coordinator, Catoctin Center for Regional Studies; Michael Powell, department chair and professor of history, Frederick Community College; Diane Weaver, independent scholar; Mark Hudson, executive director, Historical Society of Frederick County; John Howard, superintendent, Antietam National Battlefield; Jay Graybeal, Historical Society of Carroll County; Melinda Marsden, executive director, Washington County Historical Society; Liz Shatto, Historic Sites Consortium, Tourism Council of Frederick County; Janet Davis, Frederick County Planning Department, Historic Preservation Office; and Susan Trail, superintendent, Monocacy National Battlefield. The excellent working relationship that developed has carried beyond that first conference, to subsequent conferences and other initiatives, enhancing communication and collaboration.

Financial support for the conference came from a Celebration 2000 grant, Frederick Community College and the C&O Canal National Historical Park. John Howard, superintendent of the Antietam National Battlefield; Dr. Patricia Stanley, FCC president; and Dr. Suzanne Beal, academic vice president and dean of FCC, have been steady supporters of the Catoctin Center and all of its activities, including the "Millennium Crossroads" conference. FCC provided the use of its facilities and personnel, and Jeannie Winston-Muir of the Student Activities Office provided funds to allow students to attend at a discounted rate. Special thanks also go to Doug Stover for arranging a living history boat tour of the C&O Canal and to Dean Herrin for securing the keynote speakers and other presenters on the program.

In addition, this work is enhanced significantly by the images. For assistance in procuring the images, we owe a debt of gratitude to Dean Herrin of the Catoctin Center, Mark Hudson of the Historical Society of Frederick County, Mary Mannix of the Maryland Room at the C. Burr Artz Public Library, Nancy Hatcher of the Harpers Ferry National Historical Park, Terry Reimer and Kari Turner of the National Museum of Civil War Medicine, Chuck Huber of the Evangelical Lutheran Church, Barbara

Acknowledgements

Batdorf of the Frederick Presbyterian Church, Tom Gorsline of *Frederick Magazine*, Janet Davis of the Frederick County Department of Planning and Zoning, R. Christopher Goodwin, Paula Reed and Laurie Sexton. Angela Commito deserves special mention for assistance in locating and organizing the collection of these images.

To actually convert a manuscript into a format suitable for publishing requires a skill far beyond what the editors possess. For the digitization of the images, we are indebted to Michael Pritchard, Karen Defibaugh and, especially, Pierre Bowins for working their magic. Sharon Smith has generously spent hours assisting us through the intricacies of word processing, and Jaime Cardamone-May generated the index.

We are also indebted to Marie Washburn, Velma Defibaugh and Joyce Cooper of the Historical Society of Frederick County for research assistance. Amy Speck, not only coordinated the entire conference without a hitch, but also worked on this book. She contacted the authors of the different papers, collected materials and set up the initial formatting guidelines. Barbara Powell proofread the manuscript more times than she probably wanted to, but her insights significantly improved the work. Rebecca Miller became our reliable third pair of eyes, serving as copyeditor. Jessica Cannon was indispensable in typing the edits, identifying images and putting the manuscript together. Finally, we owe a debt of thanks to Jason Chasteen, Julie Hiester and the staff at The History Press for their patience and encouragement. Any mistakes are, of course, ours.

INTRODUCTION

This project evolved from several sources. The Catoctin Center for Regional Studies was created in 1998 to serve the history and research needs of the Mid-Maryland region, which consists of Washington, Frederick and Carroll Counties, and its surrounding environs. This area has served as a crossroads throughout American history. In the colonial period, immigrants crossed Pennsylvania and came down the valleys surrounding the Catoctin and Blue Ridge Mountains to settle homesteads. In the nineteenth century, major transportation routes, such as the National Road, C&O Canal and B&O Railroad, bisected the region. Both Confederate and Union armies marched through the area during the Civil War and fought battles here. The twentieth century ushered in changes such as Interstates 70 and 270, Fort Detrick, the formation of several state and national parks and the clash of development and preservation interests.

The Catoctin Center was organized under the auspices of Frederick Community College (FCC) and the National Park Service, and is housed on the college's campus. Dean Herrin, Michael Powell and Diane Weaver formed the initial steering committee, and Bruce Thompson joined one year later. One of the projects envisioned for the center was to host a conference on the region focusing on historical values and research in the community. In late 1999, the dean of FCC, Suzanne Beal, volunteered the college to host a conference as part of the statewide "Millennium 2000" celebration. The Catoctin Center was the logical choice for fulfilling this pledge.

In discussing the format of the conference, we decided not to have an organizing theme, but to accept quality papers for presentation so long as

Mid-Maryland: A Crossroads of History

they addressed important issues about the region. We found, however, that the papers seemed to organize themselves along certain themes. As we read the papers and listened to the presentations, we were constantly amazed at their quality. Historians, both professional and amateur, were exploring important aspects of our region's history and culture. Furthermore, with the development pressure on the region from the greater Baltimore/Washington area, it seemed that our history and culture were becoming more important, as much of what was familiar is becoming lost to the encroaching development and metropolitan lifestyle.

This publication of selected papers from the 2000 conference is intended to meet several needs in our community. First, it is a research outlet for many of the competent historians interested in our region and we hope historians and preservationists of the area will find much in this book that is enlightening and useful. This work is also intended for those in our community and beyond who hold a general interest in our history and culture. All cultures undergo change and transformation; what is striking about the region of Mid-Maryland is the rapidity with which this change is occurring. This collection provides a window through which to glimpse some of the changes and to examine who we are through the lenses of where we have been.

African American History

It's good to know your past. Because when you know your past, then you really got a good appreciation for where you are, where you hope to go. But if you don't know the past, sometimes you don't have any dreams.[1]

Interest in African American history has exploded in recent years. Scholars have found heretofore hidden voices that provide not only insight to the culture and community of one group of people but also a unique perspective on American history. African Americans in Mid-Maryland have a rich history. The first African Americans in the region arrived by at least the 1720s. Germans moving into the area spoke of African Americans and Native Americans living together in the mountains. The English settlers brought slaves with them and set up plantations in the eastern and southern parts of Frederick County. After the Civil War, freedman communities formed where these plantations had once operated. Their story is one of adaptation and survival, resistance and struggle, tradition and change. The papers in this section focus on the efforts of African Americans to gain their freedom—be it from slavery or segregation.

Cheryl Fox explores the story of runaway slaves in eighteenth-century Maryland. Through newspaper advertisements, she found that running away was a fairly common activity. While working for their masters, slaves and indentured servants gained knowledge of their surroundings and made contacts with other slaves and servants. When the time was right, they would steal away and hide for a few days with the aid of their contacts to renegotiate the "terms of their bondage," including the right to hire themselves out.

Mid-Maryland: A Crossroads of History

Sometimes, however, slaves would use their network of contacts to attempt to escape. Early in the eighteenth century, escaping to an Indian settlement was an option; later, runaway slaves attempted to pass as free men and women in self-sustaining African American communities.

Frederick Douglass's escape from slavery in Maryland and subsequent career as an abolitionist in the North is fairly well known. Yet, there were others. Jim Pembroke was a former slave from Washington County who changed his name to James W.C. Pennington and became a "gifted minister, abolitionist and intellectual." Dean Herrin traces Pennington's development from slave to abolitionist, finding that he drew upon his experiences as a slave to free himself mentally and spiritually.

Bruce Thompson jumps to the civil rights struggle in the twentieth century. The NAACP (National Association for the Advancement of Colored People) implemented a strategy under Charles Houston to attack the legal basis of segregation. One of the campaigns was the fight to equalize black teachers' salaries with white teachers' salaries. Howard Pindell supported the teachers' salary fight in Frederick County but lost his job as principal of Lincoln High School for his efforts. The other teachers accepted a partial raise and dropped the matter for fear of further reprisals. The NAACP depended on grassroots support from African American communities, yet, white resistance and black reluctance stalled the early civil rights movement in Frederick County.

All three essays show that African Americans were active agents in seeking their own freedom. Similarly, many whites resisted these efforts. This dynamic tension between the races is one of the paradoxical ironies of the Free State and American history.[2]

"I Went Down to the Crossroads":

Runaway Slave Strategies of Colonial and Early Federal-era Maryland African Americans

Cheryl Fox

When Robert Johnson sang of going "down to the crossroads" in the early part of this century, he felt himself sinking and hoped he would find salvation at the crossroads. In African American cultural tradition, the crossroads, or any place where two paths meet, can be a place of prayer and sacrifice and a potential source of power.[1] This paper will look at instances when enslaved Africans and African Americans in the late eighteenth century ventured to the crossroads of Maryland to obtain power over their labor and, more importantly, power over themselves. The bargains they struck for freedom were varied, but the singular desire to build communities apart from European cultural groups characterized the reported behavior of African Americans from their earliest presence in the Chesapeake region.

Runaway slave ads in the *Maryland Gazette*, 1745–60, and the *Baltimore Journal and General Advertiser*, 1755–85, reveal some of the strategies slaves employed to build networks to escape bondage.[2] They cannot, however, be considered representative of the runaway population, because not all slave owners chose

Pictured above: Runaway slave. *Courtesy of the Photographs and Prints Division, Schomburg Center for Research in Black Culture, The New York Public Library, Astor, Lenox and Tilden Foundations.*

Mid-Maryland: A Crossroads of History

to advertise their runaways and those that did frequently delayed advertising due to the expense, the expectation that the slaves would eventually return or the probability that they could be located in the vicinity. For example, a slave owner in Upper Marlborough, Prince George's County, advertised more than six months after a couple had escaped: "[O]n the 24th of February last, two Negroes, viz. a Man and a Woman; the Man is a lusty well made Fellow; the Woman a tall slim Wench, full Eyed: They have carried sundry Cloathes with them." Although their owner suspected them "harboured by the Negro Quarters," he offered a greater reward if the pair was "taken over Manockesy," on Maryland's western frontier.[3]

As in the above case, owners frequently suspected slaves of remaining in the area. In 1779, "a NEGRO MAN, named Jem, about 30" escaped. The owner stated that he had "hitherto forborne advertising him, thinking he was lurking in the neighbourhood, and would soon return home of his own accord. When he went off, he had an iron collar, which was put on him to keep him at home, but probably is, ere this, taken off." Like many escaped slaves, Jem ran to his former home, probably in an effort to reunite with his family or kin group. The advertisement continued, "[a]s my late father bought the said Jem of Mr. Richard Owings, son of Samuel, and he of Mr. Charles Wells, Sen. he may be lurking near their houses."[4] Advertisements such as these demonstrated the strong desire among runaways to develop and nurture family and kinship bonds, and were evident even in the earliest descriptions of Africans and African Americans in Maryland.

The reality of bondage did not prevent slaves from attempting to build communities among others of African or African American origin, which might provide networks through which slaves could escape and remain at large. Governor Francis Nicholson reported in 1698 that "[t]here has been imported this summer about four hundred and seventy odd Negros, viz. 396 in one ship directly from Guiny. 50 from Virginy, which came thither in a ship from Barbadoes: and few others from other places." His description revealed the origins of Maryland slaves in the colonial and early federal eras: a majority directly from Africa, a smaller portion from the Caribbean and still fewer from the southern colonies. Large groups of slaves arrived in slave ships, but many others came to the Chesapeake in small numbers on ships not dedicated to carrying slaves. Nicholson worried that there was little authorities could do to prevent strong relationships forming among even a widely dispersed population. Nicholson warned that "[slaves] might make great disturbances, if not a Rebellion: because these are very open Countrys, and they may have easy Communication with one another near the Falls of Potomock." He also observed that the "common practice is on Saturday nights and Sundays and on 2 or 3 days in Christmas, Easter, & Whitsontide, [slaves] go and see one an other, tho at 30 or 40 miles distance. I have several times both in Virginy and [Maryland] met Negros both single, and six or 7 in Company in the night time."[5]

The Maryland General Assembly sought to outlaw this independent behavior, but the necessity of planters to trade and communicate among widely separated plantations and quarters led to a continuation of the practices that enabled slaves to become familiar with the region's geography. Slaves delivered and traded goods throughout the region, thereby obtaining access to money and knowledge of the landscape. Slaves also developed relationships and established family and kinship groups throughout the region. It was through these networks that slaves could escape and sometimes remain at large.

An early effort to curtail these activities was passed in 1695. In this "Act Restraining the frequent Assembleing of Negroes within this Province," lawmakers decried the danger "attending the continual concourse of Negroes on Sabboth & holy days meeting in great numbers." They feared that slaves would challenge the system of slavery by bartering goods and "conspriring & proposeing waies & means for the gaining of their liberty & freedom which must inevitably end in Insurrection."[6]

The knowledge slaves gained through travel between quarters, and as they brought goods to market, facilitated their escape. At the same time, the common sight of slaves and free African Americans traveling throughout the region led to a degree of anonymity for runaways. For example, Kate ran away in 1756 from Henry Threlkeld, "near George-Town on Rock-Creek," which was then Frederick County. Described as a "Mulatto Woman Slave," Kate was "pretty well dressed," and "may sometimes pass for a free Woman where she is not known to be otherwise." According to Threlkeld, she had belonged to Benjamin Lane in Anne Arundel County, but within six months of her sale and movement to Frederick County, she stole a horse and escaped. Threlkeld "supposed she [was] secreted by a Mulatto Slave called Jemmy (a Carpenter by Trade), belonging to Mr. Thomas Sprigg, on West-River," near Annapolis and probably her former home, about twenty-five miles away. She escaped, according to the advertisement,

> *with the Assistance and Contrivance of some other Slaves in the neighbourhood where she was bought, who (it seems she has bragg'd) had promised to conceal her whenever she would run away from me. I understand she has been a great Rambler, and is well known in Calvert and Anne-Arundel*

Mid-Maryland: A Crossroads of History

Counties, besides other parts of the Country. She may indulge herself a little visiting her old Acquaintance; but is most probable she will spend the greater Part of her Time with or near wherever the aforesaid Mulatto Slave of Mr. Sprigg's may be at Work.[7]

Kate evidently earned her reputation as a "great rambler," but her ability to develop networks of kin among disparate quarters, and her inclination to return to familiar areas, are common themes among runaways.

Slave runaways of the colonial era were unlikely to ally themselves with members of the tiny free African American population in the Chesapeake region. Ira Berlin has noted that this group of free African Americans, the charter generation, was the product of the Atlantic slave trade and had Spanish or Portuguese origins. Later slaves arriving in the Chesapeake were Africans, not related by blood or language to the free population at that time.[8] Fugitive slaves with ties to the free population did not become a significant factor in slave resistance until the nineteenth century.

In fact, prior to the Revolution, the free African American population was perceived "both by themselves and the white majority as a class of people existing apart from the rest of the black population."[9] But when Revolutionary War liberation fervor brought with it a wave of manumissions in Maryland, the resulting larger population of free African Americans, with a new racial and cultural composition, was far less willing or able to disassociate themselves from slaves because of family ties.

Cooperation of runaways across racial lines can be attributed to family and kin group ties formed as slaves and indentured servants served side by side. Fragmentary evidence suggests that during the colonial era, one quarter to one third of illegitimate children born to white women had fathers of African descent.[10] Colonial slaves often formed alliances with white indentured servants who shared a common social station. Based on a comparative analysis of runaway ads of both slaves and indentured servants, Lelsey-Alicia Delahunty concludes that, "[i]n the [*Maryland*] *Gazette*, the white planter elite appears to be at the top of a small body of white entrepreneurs and merchants, all over a mass of unfree white, black, and mulatto laborers." Patterns in clothing reported in these ads occurred not "along racial lines, but included ethnic, bound servitude, and economic factors." Delahunty interprets this as an indication that "most unfree laboring men in the Chesapeake belonged to, and were treated as a monolithic underclass."[11]

Many, if not most, European immigrants to the colonies arrived in some form of bound servitude. Although the opportunity for freedom existed for these term servants in theory, many indentured servants in fact faced perpetual bound servitude due to financial limitations. Many servants were forced to bind themselves to additional terms and sometimes a literal life servitude was imposed on indentured servants such as in the following case:

> *June 2, 1746. Whereas, a certain Robert Impey, hath this Day, indented* [indentured] *himself a Servant unto me the Subscriber, for and during the Term of his natural Life; These are therefore to forewarn all manner of Persons from Dealing with the said Robert Impey, upon pain of incurring the Penalties inflicted by the Act of Assembly in Such Cases made and provided. Thomas Sparrow.*[12]

The affiliation among laborers of diverse backgrounds is seen in the following example of an escaped trio from Frederick County in 1775: "Ran away last night…the three following persons, viz. THOMAS TURNER, an Irish indentured servant…JOHN HOW, a convict…HANNAH, a Negro woman, about 20, 5'3 or 4" high and very lusty." Hannah appears to have intended to be gone quite a while, as she

> [h]*ad on and took with her, a new stampt cotton gown, black quilted petticoat, one white shift, two white aprons, one pair of thread stockings, one pair white cotton ditto, two white handkerchiefs, two check aprons, one country linen do., a striped holland petticoat, calico jacket, a pair of shoes with plated buckles, and sundry other things two* [sic] *tedious to mention.*[13]

The few scattered remaining Indian settlements in Maryland provided another opportunity for slaves seeking to escape. Maroon colonies like those in South America, the Caribbean or even the Deep South have not been recorded in the Chesapeake region, but it is well documented that this type of resistance was practiced by Maryland slaves. In 1652, the Maryland General Assembly forged "articles of peace and friendship" with the Susquehanna Indians, partly to stem the tide of runaway slaves (and servants) who left the colony for the frontier. In this treaty, the Indians promised to return any "people or servants belonging to the English."[14]

Another treaty was sought in 1722 in response to "certain Negro Slaves who for some time past have been entertain'd at [Shawan or Shuano] Indian Towns upon [the] Potomac River." Emissary Charles Anderson was instructed by the General Assembly to offer the Indians "two Stroud [Match Coat]s and a Gun," if they "will send down those Negro people that have lived among them."[15] In 1726, a petition to the Upper House was made for legislation designed to discourage "several Convicts having lately attempted (by way of Monokosey) to make their Escapes and may probably seduce others to follow their Example and also that Sundry negroes have and may by the same way make their Escape to the Shuano town."[16] This settlement, on the western edge of Prince George's County, continued at least a few years, as that county's court records for 1728 include the deposition of Eleanor Cushoca, in which she recounts a discussion among slaves from several plantations regarding the return of "a negro man of John Miller's" from "the Indians at Monocacy Mountains whose name was Harry."[17] Harry had apparently returned to try to persuade other slaves to join the settlement.

Indians on the frontier continued to present a problem, however, and the general anxiety about them arose in connection with the 1739–40 slave conspiracy in Prince George's County. The members of the General Assembly wrote to the British, informing them of "the Danger we lately escaped from the horrid Conspiracy of Our Negroes," in part to justify a request for additional funds to arm the frontier against imminent attack by the French (who recruited both Indians and escaped slaves), Spanish, "Roman Catholics, Negroes, or any other Enemies."[18] The conspiracy involving as many as two hundred slaves was planned over eight months. Jack Ransome led the largely African group, reportedly undertaken in "their country language," to remove European settlers and unite both Eastern and Western shore Maryland as an African settlement.[19]

Indian threats to the frontier receded with the westward development of the colonies, but as late as the mid-eighteenth century, escaping to an Indian settlement was still a viable option. In 1752, an ad described a "tall thin Mulatto Slave, [who] looks very much like an Indian and will endeavor to pass for such when it suits him; he is about 38 years of age. It is imagined he is making upwards, to get amongst the Back Indians, having with him an Indian Match Coat…Henry Waggaman."[20]

Short of actual escape, many slaves effectively stole their own labor by surreptitiously hiring out their own time. John Bullen was forced to advertise in the *Maryland Gazette* in 1752 that "Whereas sundry persons within this City, have and still continue, not only frequently to deal with, but do daily employ my House Negro Fellows, in any Week they will undertake, without my license for so doing, to the great detriment and neglect of my business."[21]

Having marketable skills greatly increased the odds of remaining free; and while, in general, fewer slaves were practicing trades in the eighteenth as opposed to the seventeenth century, Africans and African Americans did participate to a limited extent in a variety of trades and even professional occupations. One such was the slave who escaped from Samuel Norwood, living near the head of Patapsco River. According to Norwood, "he can read and write, and it is supposed he will endeavor to pass for a Freeman and a Doctor."[22] Another slave expected to try to pass for free and work in an urban area was Dick, whose owner was "informed he goes by the name of Jack Simpson, and has a forg'd Pass, pretending he has served as a Mulatto 31 years, agreeable to the laws of the Colony." He was "by Trade a compleat Wheelwright, and so much of a Smith, as to make the Nails, and shoe those he makes. He is likewise a good Cooper, Sawyer, and House-Carpenter, and has also been employed in Small craft by Water." His owner in Dumfries expected that his experience living in Fredericksburg, and other "public places," would have helped him learn how to get around in the region and allowed him to build a network of acquaintances, by which means he might be "conveyed out of this Colony."[23]

As the above ad suggests, slaves and indentured servants bargained and negotiated with slave owners to modify the terms of their bondage. Slaves were frequently granted permission to hire out their labor, but it could be just as easily withdrawn. A few slaves had success in negotiating an end to their service, either through hiring out their time to pay an agreed upon fee, or by in effect revising their status to one of a term servant. The ability to successfully negotiate such an arrangement depended upon knowledge gained through work and interaction with whites. No less important for slaves seeking freedom was luck and the determination to continually attempt to escape.

With the onset of the Revolutionary War, the colonists feared mass escape of slaves to the British military. News of the possibility of freedom spread among slaves in Maryland. In 1777, a slave owner sought

> *two following Negro men. PERTH, a likely strong fellow, born in this country, about 28 years, 5 feet 8 or 9 inches high...CATO, a likely fellow, African born, about the same age and height of Perth, not so strong made, of a lighter complexion...The above Negroes had assumed the names of Daniel Williams and Daniel Shaw, and endeavoured to enlist in the Continental service at York-Town, Pennsylvania, where they were committed to gaol, but escaped therefrom...it is supposed they will endeavour to enlist either in the land or sea service, with a design of getting to the enemy the first opportunity. Perth has been brought up to the water, Cato as a gentleman's servant, can shave and dress hair, and has been in Philadelphia and New-York.*[24]

Mid-Maryland: A Crossroads of History

Escaped slaves held positions in the British army or navy, but would also have sought opportunities to work in the colony camps. In 1778, for example, "three Negro men, viz. JOE, JEM, and SAURAH…a Guinea Negro…Negro Joe and Saurah did live, a few months past, at Mr. Young's force, on French Creek, Pennsylvania State. It is probable that those Negroes have made for camp and are in the army."[25]

As the war progressed, all of the Southern states increased patrols, established local guard units, removed slaves from proximity to British forces and imposed severe punishments on would-be defectors. But these actions could not prevent several thousand slaves from seeking service and freedom with the British. Troop movements in the area brought another opportunity for slaves to escape. In 1778, for example,

> *BENJAMIN HARWOOD, a Mulatto, the son of a white man…The last I hear of him, he was near the Falls of James river, a few miles behind a brigade of wagons returning from the southward to Frederick county, in the state of Maryland, and pretended to belong to some person with those waggons. I have also been informed, that he several times applied to the waggon-master (a Mr. Goode) to enlist him a soldier, insisting that he was a free man.*[26]

In June 1779, British General Sir Henry Clinton officially promised to emancipate any male slaves who escaped to join the British militia. This promise surely influenced would-be slave runaways such as "…a dark MULATTO MAN, named JACK, about 40 years age…He is an artful fellow and it is suspected will (as he has before) attempt to get to the British Army…Abraham Risteau."[27]

Beginning in 1791, when the site of the new national capital was surveyed and partially cleared, Washington City became a draw both for slave owners seeking to hire out slaves they no longer needed for plantation work, as well as escaped slaves who sought the anonymity of this busy area to pass for free. Carved from Virginia and Maryland, which together held more slaves in 1800 than in the rest of the United States combined, construction in the city of Washington naturally included slave labor as a major component of its work force. Beginning in 1792, slaves hauled stone from Virginia quarries to Washington, and by 1797 the city rented 125 slaves for various occupations.[28]

The use of slaves in this manner in Washington led to the city becoming a draw for escaped slaves who had skills, such as Clem and Will of Prince George's County who "were last seen on their way to the City of Washington with their broad axes and some other tools."[29] The presence of slaves in the

> **Runaway Slave in Cuſtody of the Sheriff o Frederick County, viz.**
>
> A Negro Man, called STEPhEN, 5 feet 6 inche high, about 22 years old ; had on when commit ted, a half-worn felt-hat, with a black riband and whit metal buckle, a hunting ſhirt, great coat, nankeen o- veralls, and a pair of mockaſins. Says he belongs to Henry Frinſworth, living in Greene county, ſouth- weſtern Territory, three miles from the court houſe. And unleſs he be releaſed by his owner, he will be ſold for his jail fees, agreeably to law.
> RICHARD BUTLER, Sheriff.
> Frederick county, ſtate of Maryland,
> October 9, 1795.   1aw8t†

Advertisement for runaway slave in Frederick County that appeared in the *Federal Intelligencer and Baltimore Daily Gazette,* December 18, 1795.

workforce was initially thought to be a check on immigrant white laborers, especially the Irish, but the danger of increased numbers of slaves in the capital was soon felt. The city of Georgetown, outside of Washington City but within the Federal District, enacted an ordinance in 1795 prohibiting the congregation of more than five slaves, punishable by thirty-nine lashes and a thirteen-dollar fine.[30]

As advertisements attest, slaves regularly made use of the knowledge they gained in their service to build networks in order to escape or to pass for free and sell their own labor. Throughout the period leading up to the American Revolution and during the early Federal era, two demographic trends enhanced the ability of African Americans to build communities. The significant increase in opportunities for manumission following the Revolution enabled African Americans to buy their families out of slavery and create self-sustaining communities. At the same time, an increase in the slave population allowed enslaved African Americans to build kinship groups and communities that crossed plantation lines.

Only a tiny portion of Maryland's colonial African American population was free, but following the war the number grew significantly. By the time the Civil War began, nearly half were free. In addition to manumissions within the state, the number of free African Americans increased following Gabriel's rebellion in 1806, because Virginia free blacks were forced to leave and some came to Maryland.[31] Ironically, this trend toward freedom of African Americans in Maryland stood in stark contrast to Maryland's emerging role as an exporter of slaves. Slavery would last another half century, and some slaves would continue to respond to their bondage by running away, building communities based on family, kinship and cultural lines.

Bibliography

"An Account of the Number of Souls in the Province of Maryland in the Year 1755." *Gentlemen's Magazine* 34 (1764). MdHRG 1213-449, Peabody Library Collection of the Johns Hopkins University, Baltimore.

Aptheker, Herbert. *American Negro Slave Revolts*. New York: International Publishers, 1974.

Arnebeck, Bob. "Slaves at the Founding." http://www.geocities.com/bobarnebeck/slaves.html.

Bacon, Mary Ann. "Eighteenth-Century Annapolis." Master's thesis, Columbia University, 1943.

Baltimore Journal and General Advertiser, 1755–1780.

Berlin, Ira. *Many Thousands Gone: The First Two Centuries of Slavery in North America*. Cambridge, MA: Harvard University Press, 1998.

———. *Slaves Without Masters: The Free Negro in the Antebellum South*. New York: New Press, 1974.

Berlin, Ira and Ronald Hoffman. *Slavery and Freedom in the Age of the American Revolution*. Charlottesville: University Press of Virginia, 1983.

Council of Maryland. Proceedings of the Council of Maryland. Vols. 23 and 25. Maryland State Archives, Hall of Records, Annapolis, MD.

Curtin, Philip D. *Atlantic Slave Trade: A Census*. Madison: University of Wisconsin Press, 1969.

African American History

Davidson, Thomas E. "Free Black Landowners on the Lower Eastern Shore of Maryland, 1783–1861." Paper presented at Black Studies Conference, Baltimore, October 1982.

Delahunty, Lelsey-Alicia Bernadette. "Such as Servants Commonly Wear: The Appearance of Laboring Men and Women in the Chesapeake, as Described in the *Maryland Gazette*, 1745–1765." Master's thesis, University of Maryland, College Park, 1992.

Fields, Barbara Jeanne. *Slavery and Freedom on the Middle Ground, Maryland during the Nineteenth Century*. New Haven, CT: Yale University Press, 1985.

Gomez. Michael A. *Exchanging Our Country Marks: The Transformation of African Identities in the Colonial and Antebellum South*. Chapel Hill: University of North Carolina Press, 1998.

Hall, Robert. *Atlantic Slave Trade Revisited: The Case of Maryland*. Baltimore: University of Maryland, Baltimore County, 1989.

Joyner, Charles. *Down by the Riverside*. Chicago: University of Illinois Press, 1984.

Kulikoff, Allan. *Tobacco and Slaves: The Development of Southern Cultures in the Chesapeake, 1680–1800*. Chapel Hill: University of North Carolina Press, 1986.

Lewis, Ronald L. *Coal, Iron, and Slaves: Industrial Slavery in Maryland and Virginia, 1715–1865*. Westport, CT: Greenwood Press, 1979.

Maryland Gazette, 1745–1760.

Maryland General Assembly. Assembly Proceedings, Acts of May 1695. Vol. 38. Maryland State Archives, Hall of Records, Annapolis, MD.

———. Assembly Proceedings, Upper House. Vols. 35 and 40. Maryland State Archives, Hall of Records, Annapolis, MD.

Morgan, Philip D. *Slave Counterpoint: Black Culture in the Eighteenth-Century Chesapeake & Lowcountry*. Chapel Hill: University of North Carolina Press, 1998.

Mullin, Gerald W. *Flight and Rebellion: Slave Resistance in Eighteenth Century Virginia*. New York: Oxford University Press, 1972.

Mid-Maryland: A Crossroads of History

Quarles, Benjamin. *The Negro in the American Revolution*. Chapel Hill: University of North Carolina Press, 1961.

Riley, Elihu S. *The Ancient City: A History of Annapolis in Maryland*. Annapolis: Record Printing Office, 1887.

Thompson, Robert Farris. *Face of the Gods, Art and Alters of Africa and the African Americans*. New York: The Museum for African Art, 1993.

Walsh, Lorena S. "Slave Life, Slave Society, and Tobacco Production in the Tidewater Chesapeake 1620–1820." In *Cultivation & Culture*, edited by Ira Berlin. Charlottesville: University Press of Virginia, 1993.

Windley, Lathan A. *Runaway Slave Advertisements, 1730 to 1790: Maryland*. Vols. 2 and 4. Westport, CT: Greenwood Press, 1983.

Yentsch, Anne E. *A Chesapeake Family and Their Slaves: A Study in Historical Archaeology*. New York: Cambridge University Press, 1994.

From Slave to Abolitionist:

James W.C. Pennington of Washington County, Maryland

Dean Herrin

Sunday, October 28, 1827, was Jim Pembroke's last day in Washington County, Maryland. A slave for all of his twenty-one years, Pembroke had decided the previous day to escape. Yet, as he sat alone that Sunday morning, awaiting the right moment to leave, he hesitated and considered the difficulties of his decision. First and foremost, he was worried about his family. He would be leaving behind on the plantation not only his mother and his father, but also ten siblings, plus a beloved older brother who lived nearby. What would become of them? Pembroke was well aware that it was a custom for families of runaways to be sold to the Deep South before they had a chance to follow their kinsman. What, on the other hand, would happen to him if he failed? The consequences would no doubt be severe. Even if he managed to escape, he was unsure how to even get to Pennsylvania and freedom—he could only guess at the distance from his plantation to the state border, and he had little sense of direction, save for following the North Star. Years later, Pembroke wrote of his mental anguish that day:

James W.C. Pennington. *Courtesy of the Wesleyan University Press.*

Mid-Maryland: A Crossroads of History

How the impression came to be upon my mind I cannot tell; but there was a strange and horrifying belief that, if I did not meet the crisis that day, I should be self-doomed—that my ear would be nailed to the door post forever. The emotions of that moment I cannot fully depict. Hope, fear, dread, terror, love, sorrow, and deep melancholy were mingled in my mind together; my mental state was one of most painful distraction…[B]ut the hour was now come, and the man must act and be free, or remain a slave forever.[1]

Pembroke put a piece of bread in his pocket, looked around his slave quarters one last time, and left behind Washington County and slavery forever.

Jim Pembroke's story is one of the great slave narratives of American history. After his escape, Pembroke changed his name to James William Charles Pennington, and against all odds, became one of the most distinguished and respected of all African American leaders of the nineteenth century.[2] We know about his early life as a slave primarily from his autobiography, published in 1849 as *The Fugitive Blacksmith or Events in the History of James W.C. Pennington.*[3] While Pennington's life as an abolitionist and public figure is well known, few have examined his early years in Maryland. His story is certainly inspirational as one man's successful struggle against an evil institution, but it also tells us much about slavery and early African American history in Mid-Maryland, as well as aspects of the cultural world of the antebellum white planter class in the region. His experiences in Washington County were part and parcel of the influences that transformed Jim Pembroke the slave into James W.C. Pennington the gifted minister, abolitionist and intellectual.

Pennington was born circa 1807 in Queen Anne's County on the Eastern Shore of Maryland. His mother, Nelly Pembroke, and therefore Jim, were slaves to James Tilghman, a judge on Maryland's Court of Appeals and the state's first attorney general. Pennington's father, Bazil, was owned by a different slaveholder on a nearby plantation. When James Tilghman died in 1809, his will was administered by his eldest surviving son, Frisby Tilghman. Several years earlier, Frisby had emigrated from Queen Anne's County to Washington County in Mid-Maryland, a wheat-growing region that was one of the most rapidly expanding sections of the state. After settling his father's affairs, Frisby Tilghman returned to his Washington County estate Rockland with Nelly and her two sons, Robert and Jim. Pennington's father was thus separated from his family by over two hundred miles, but Tilghman soon thereafter purchased Bazil and brought him also to Rockland.[4]

Pennington did not know it at the time of course, but he had been inherited by one of Washington County's leading citizens. Frisby Tilghman had once studied to be a doctor, but after marrying into a prominent local family, the Ringgolds, he became a wheat farmer and an active participant in the civic life of his adopted region. He represented Washington County four times in Maryland's House of Delegates, served as a justice in the county's Orphans Court, formed and commanded a local militia company, helped to found the first agricultural society in the county as well as an academy in Hagerstown, championed the building of the Chesapeake & Ohio Canal and other internal improvements in the region, served on the board of directors of local banks and was influential as one of the more progressive farmers in the region.[5]

Pennington recalled in his memoirs that Tilghman normally displayed a kind disposition, but was a strict disciplinarian with his slaves and was ever vigilant to extinguish any sign of autonomy from them. For example, Tilghman was an instigator of several laws in the county concerning the control of slaves, including one that prohibited slaves from traveling over a certain number of miles from their plantation on Sundays, the day they were traditionally allowed to visit family members on nearby plantations. He also once had authorities disband a local Sunday school for free blacks that had been established by Methodist and Lutheran churches lest, according to Pennington, "the slaves should get some benefit of it." Tilghman's treatment of Pennington and his family sparked Pennington's later determination to flee.[6]

As a young boy, Pennington helped his parents as much as he could around the plantation, until approximately age eight or nine, when he and his older brother Robert were hired out by Tilghman to learn trades. As in many other slave areas, there was a custom in the region for slave owners to apprentice a few of their young slaves to tradesmen, in order for the slaves to learn a skill that could later be used on the plantation. Pennington was placed with a stonemason in Hagerstown, six miles from Tilghman's plantation. Pennington's brother Robert was apprenticed to a different tradesman in the same town, and since neither Pennington's nor his brother's employer were slave owners themselves, the two boys enjoyed for a brief time relative freedom. Pennington stayed with the stonemason for about three years and then returned home. His new skills were immediately employed in helping to erect a new blacksmith shop for the plantation. Tilghman's blacksmith was a slave who had been apprenticed to learn his trade just as Pennington had, and Pennington was placed in the new shop to learn the craft. He worked as a blacksmith on Tilghman's plantation for nine years and took great pride in his work. He wrote in his autobiography that this craftsman's pride was one of the things that reconciled him so long to being a slave: "I sought to distinguish myself in the finer branches of the business by invention and finish; I frequently tried my hand at making guns and pistols, putting blades in penknives, making fancy hammers, hatchets, swordcanes, etc., etc."[7]

But Pennington found little else in the life of a slave to give him satisfaction. In *The Fugitive Blacksmith*, he described aspects of a slave's life in Washington County. Compared with the tobacco-growing regions of eastern Maryland, western Maryland had comparatively fewer slaves. Still, at about the time Pennington was brought to Washington County, there were over 2,600 people in bondage in the county, and that number increased to over 3,200 by 1820. In that year, slaves accounted for 14 percent of Washington County's total population, which was comparable to neighboring Frederick County, where slaves made up 16 percent of the population. By comparison, slaves composed 26 percent of the population for the entire state. The number of slaves in Washington County declined thereafter until slavery was abolished in the state in 1864. The number of free blacks in the county, on the other hand, increased until, in 1860, on the eve of the Civil War, the number of free blacks outnumbered enslaved blacks.[8]

Slavery, however, was manifested in Washington County through more than just the numbers of slaves. According to Thomas J.C. Williams's *History of Washington County, Maryland*, Hagerstown was always a noted slave market—slave catchers from throughout the Southern states lurked in the county in attempts to catch fugitive slaves trying to escape to Pennsylvania. Once caught, many of these slaves were then sold at auction in Hagerstown to buyers from the Deep South. In his three years in Hagerstown, Pennington likely witnessed a few of these auctions.[9]

The prevailing attitude toward slavery in Washington County was recounted by Pennington in his retelling of the Gruber trial of 1819. Jacob Gruber was a Pennsylvania minister who, at a camp meeting near Tilghman's Rockland estate in 1818, delivered a sermon in which several Washington County slave owners accused him of inciting slaves to rebel against their masters. Gruber was successfully defended, however, by Roger Brooke Taney, then a lawyer in Frederick County and, in one of history's interesting ironies, the future author of the *Dred Scott* decision, where he ruled that slaves were property only, and could never be citizens. Pennington claimed that his owner, Frisby Tilghman, was one of the planters responsible for Gruber's arrest. He also recounted an 1848 meeting with a slave from the region who still remembered Gruber's sermon.[10]

Pennington recalled in his book numerous details of how slaves in Washington County lived, touching upon foodways, religion and clothing, for example, but he was understandably more interested in describing for readers the cruelties of slavery. Remember that Pennington wrote his autobiography in 1849, when slavery was still legal. In the preface of his book, he particularly criticized people who spoke of a "mild" form of slavery.

> *My feelings are always outraged when I hear them speak of "kind masters," "Christian masters," "the mildest form of slavery," "well fed and clothed slaves," as extenuations of slavery; I am satisfied they either mean to pervert the truth, or they do not know what they say. The being of slavery, its soul and body, lives and moves in the chattel principle, the property principle, the bill of sale principle; the cart-whip, starvation, and nakedness, are its inevitable consequences to a greater or less extent.*[11]

Pennington cited many examples throughout his book to illustrate the cruelty and barbarity of slavery, even of the so-called mild kind. He witnessed slave children sold from the plantation to the Deep South, men and women flogged, a slave struck with a pitchfork by an overseer and slaves shot. One slave tried to run from one of Frisby Tilghman's overseers who was preparing to beat him with a club. The overseer grabbed a gun and shot the slave, hitting him in the legs. The slave managed to hide in the nearby woods, but the pain forced him to surrender that night. Tilghman did not immediately tend to his wounds, but had him locked up that night, and in the morning had the overseer tie him down and flog him—only then did Tilghman pick the shot out of the slave's leg. In another example, one of Tilghman's sons desired a young slave woman on the plantation, "for no honorable purposes," claimed Pennington. In order to save the honor of the son, Tilghman sold the slave to a buyer from Georgia, despite the pleadings of her parents to allow them to arrange a local sale.[12]

Pennington and his family did not escape the wrath of Tilghman and his overseers either; one particular incident produced a turning point in Pennington's conception of himself and his situation. Tilghman allowed his slaves who had families on other nearby plantations to leave on Saturday night to go to their families, providing they returned to their plantations by early Monday morning. On one particular Monday, Tilghman was enraged upon discovering that three of his field hands had failed to return to the property. Pennington's father was tending a lamb that morning on the plantation, and Tilghman directed his anger at Bazil. When Bazil replied in a way that Tilghman felt was insolent, he took out a cowhide whip and, in Pennington's words:

> *fell upon him with most savage cruelty, and inflicted fifteen or twenty severe stripes with all his strength, over his shoulders and the small of his back. As he raised himself upon his toes, and gave the last stripe, he said, "by the *** I will make you know that I am master of your tongue as well as of your time!"*

Pennington was near enough to "hear, see, and even count the savage stripes inflicted upon" his father.[13]

Pennington recalled that this incident created "an open rupture" within his family, as "each member felt the deep insult that had been inflicted upon our head: the spirit of the whole family was roused; we talked of it in our nightly gatherings, and showed it in our daily melancholy aspect." Yet, did this cause Tilghman to regret his actions? On the contrary, "The oppressor saw this, and with the heartlessness that was in perfect keeping with the first insult, commenced a series of tauntings, threatenings, and insinuations, with a view to crush the spirit of the whole family."[14]

Pennington's response was a portent of his later actions. "Although it was some time after this event before I took the decisive step, yet in my mind and spirit, I never was a *Slave* after it." He particularly never forgot the symbolism in the stark contrast between the gentleness of his father's caring for the lamb and the cruelty of Tilghman. Pennington now despised Tilghman, and the slave owner, knowing this, sought incidents in which he could punish the young man.[15]

Soon afterward, Pennington made his decision to emancipate himself by running away. On the afternoon of October 28, 1827, he left Rockland as if to visit his brother in Hagerstown. As night was falling, he kept walking, thinking only of freedom. In his story, Pennington remembered his feelings that night:

> *I felt like a mariner who has gotten his ship outside of the harbor and has spread his sails to the breeze. The cargo is on board—the ship is cleared—and the voyage I must make; besides, this being my first night, almost everything will depend upon my clearing the coast before the day dawns. In order to do this my flight must be rapid. I therefore set forth in sorrowful earnest, only now and then I was cheered by the wild hope, that I should somewhere and at some time be free.*[16]

Unfortunately, Pennington's fears about direction were well founded, for after two nights of walking, hiding in cornfields and eating little, he found himself at a toll gate of the National Pike, only eighteen miles from Baltimore.

> **200 Dollars Reward.**
>
> RAN AWAY from the subscriber living near Hagers-town, Washington county, Md. on Monday the twenty-ninth of October, a negro man named JAMES PEMBROOK, about 21 years of age, five feet five inches high, very black, square & clumsily made; has a down look, prominent and reddish eyes, and mumbles or talks with his teeth closed, can read, and I believe write, is an excellent blacksmith, and pretty good rough carpenter; he received shortly before he absconded, a pretty severe cut from his axe on the inside of his right leg. Any person who will take up and secure him in the jail of Hagers-town shall receive the above reward.
>
> FRISBY TILGHMAN.
> November 1. 1—tf.

Advertisement of Pennington as a runaway slave as found in *The Torch Light and Public Advertiser* (Hagerstown, MD), December 13, 1827. Courtesy of the Washington County Free Library.

Much to his dismay, he realized he had traveled east instead of north. But his troubles were only beginning. Pennington was soon captured near Reisterstown by a local farmer who suspected him of being a runaway. He managed to buy himself time by claiming to have been part of a gang of slaves that had contracted smallpox. Eventually he found a way to escape, and continued on his journey to Pennsylvania. Six days after leaving Washington County, he finally entered Pennsylvania near Littlestown in Adams County. There he was taken in by William and Phoebe Wright, a local Quaker family, and sheltered for six months.[17]

Upon discovering Pennington's departure, Frisby Tilghman immediately placed an advertisement in the local papers. Tilghman was none too happy to lose a slave so skilled as Pennington. His ad offered a $200 reward for Pennington, and described him as, "about 21 years of age, five feet, five inches high, very black, square & clumsily made, has a down look, prominent and reddish eyes, and mumbles or talks with his teeth closed, can read, and I believe write, is an excellent blacksmith, and pretty good rough carpenter." Tilghman did not give up looking for Pennington. Over a year later Tilghman was still placing ads in newspapers in Lancaster and Philadelphia looking for his fugitive blacksmith.[18]

William Wright was a former schoolmaster, and while Pennington stayed in Littlestown, Wright began teaching Pennington how to read and write. As a slave, Pennington had spent many Sundays in his blacksmith shop, secretly studying the writing in the daybook kept by the shop's overseer. He had even fashioned a crude steel pen and had made ink from berries to practice writing. An avid learner, he always lamented what slavery had deprived him:

> *There is one sin that slavery committed against me which I never can forgive. It robbed me of my education; the injury is irreparable; I feel the embarrassment more seriously now than I ever did before. It cost me two years' hard labor, after I fled, to unshackle my mind; it was three years before I had purged my language of slavery's idioms; it was four years before I had thrown off the crouching aspect of slavery.*[19]

Pennington soon left the Wrights, as Littlestown was too near the Maryland border, and he eventually arrived in New York City, and the beginning of a long career as a minister, teacher, abolitionist, writer and international figure. One historian has written that Pennington was "one of the most distinguished of all fugitives from bondage," and another referred to him as "one of the most educated and literate black men of his time."

Pennington became a minister in Presbyterian churches in New York and Hartford, was elected a delegate to several international abolition conventions, founded the American Missionary Association, wrote one of the first histories of Africans in America in 1841, lectured widely, led the struggle to desegregate New York City's public transit system, fought for the right of blacks to vote and remained active in the Underground Railroad. In 1849, the University of Heidelberg awarded Pennington a Doctor of Divinity degree in honor of his achievements. His autobiography, also first published in 1849, has been called by a historian one of the ten most important slave narratives, and, as has been noted by literary historians, provided Mark Twain with several good ideas. *The Fugitive Blacksmith* went through three editions in eleven months, selling over six thousand copies.[20]

The title of Pennington's book was apt, for he was technically still a fugitive in 1849. Pennington's friends had tried earlier in the 1840s to purchase his freedom and that of his parents from Tilghman, but negotiations had failed. With the passage of the Fugitive Slave Law in 1850, which placed new dangers on all runaways, Pennington's very freedom was at stake. Frisby Tilghman died in 1847, and the administrator of his estate declared that $150 would buy Pennington's freedom. Abolitionists in Scotland raised the money, and in June of 1851, Pennington was technically a free man for the first time in his life.[21]

Many members of his family were not so fortunate. Several were sold farther south, a few managed to eventually escape to Canada, and others remained slaves in Washington County. One brother, Stephen, along with his two sons, ran away from his Sharpsburg, Maryland, owner in 1854. Through the Underground Railroad network, they made their way to Pennington in New York. But, slave catchers were on their trail, and Stephen and his sons were captured after less than twenty-four hours in the city. Stephen's two sons were immediately sold to a North Carolina lumber merchant, but Pennington was able to raise enough money to eventually purchase Stephen.[22]

Prior to Frisby Tilghman's death, Pennington wrote a remarkable letter to his former owner. In this letter from 1844, Pennington turned the slave/master relationship on its head. Pennington warned Tilghman that he was an old man and would probably die soon, and he would have to stand "at the awful bar of the impartial Judge." He reminded his former owner that he would meet his former slaves, including Pennington, at that bar.

> *They will all meet you at that bar. Uncle James True, Charles Cooper, Aunt Jenny, and the native Africans; Jeremiah, London, and Donmore, have already gone ahead, and only wait your arrival—Sir, I shall meet you there. The account between us for the first twenty years of my life, will have a definite character upon which one or the other will be able to make out a case.*[23]

Most significantly, Pennington wrote, "I called you master when I was with you from the mere force of circumstances; but I never regarded you as my master." Pennington had emancipated himself.[24]

Bibliography

"An Act for the Relief of Frisby Tilghman of Washington County." Chap. 67 in *Laws Made and Passed by the General Assembly of the State of Maryland*. Annapolis: William M'Neir, 1842.

Blackett, R.J.M. *Beating Against the Barriers, Biographical Essays in Nineteenth-Century Afro-American History*. Baton Rouge: Louisiana State University Press, 1986.

Boles, John B. "Tension in a Slave Society: The Trial of the Reverend Jacob Gruber." *Southern Studies* 18 (Summer, 1979): 179–97.

Mid-Maryland: A Crossroads of History

(Hagerstown, MD) *Torchlight and Public Advertiser*. December 13, 1827, and February 5, 1829.

Hooker, John. *Some Reminiscences of a Long Life*. Hartford, CT: Belknap & Warfield, 1899.

Jacobs, Gary. "Slavery in Washington County, Maryland." Honors paper, Hood College, 1978.

MacKethan, Lucinda H. "Huck Finn and the Slave Narratives." *Southern Review* 20 (April 1984): 247–64.

Pennington, James W.C. *The Fugitive Blacksmith or Events in the History of James W.C. Pennington*. 3rd ed. (1850). Reprinted in Arna Bontemps. *Great Slave Narratives*. Boston: Beacon Press, 1969.

Scharf, J. Thomas. *History of Western Maryland*. 2 vols. 1882. Reprint, Baltimore: Regional Publishing Co., 1968.

Still, William. *The Underground Railroad*. 1872. Reprint, New York: Arno, 1968.

Strickland, W.P. *The Life of Jacob Gruber*. New York: Carlton & Porter, 1860.

Strother, Horatio T. *The Underground Railroad in Connecticut*. Middletown, CT: Wesleyan University, 1962.

Taylor, Yuval, ed. *I Was Born a Slave, An Anthology of Classic Slave Narratives, Volume Two, 1849–1866*. Chicago: Lawrence Hill, 1999.

Thomas, Herman E. *James W.C. Pennington, African American Churchman and Abolitionist*. New York: Garland, 1995.

Williams, Thomas J.C. *History of Washington County, Maryland*. 1906. Reprint, Baltimore: Clearfield Co., 1992.

Segregated Salaries:

The Struggle to Equalize Teachers' Salaries in Frederick County

Bruce A. Thompson

Usually the civil rights movement evokes images of the dramatic events from 1954 to 1965—Rosa Parks on a bus in Montgomery, Alabama; students sitting-in at department store lunch counters; or Martin Luther King Jr., delivering his "I have a dream" speech at the march on Washington. Never does anyone ever mention Frederick, Maryland, and seldom do scholars focus on the early civil rights movement from 1935 to 1954. Yet, for a few months in 1938, Frederick and the early civil rights movement crossed paths. The black schoolteachers in the county sought salaries equal to their white counterparts. Their petition for salary equity—as part of a larger campaign launched by Charles Houston of the National Association for the Advancement of Colored People (NAACP) to abolish segregation—would fall on deaf ears. In fact, white officials in Frederick County were successful in preserving segregated teacher salaries until 1955. This episode shows some of the challenges that confronted the early civil rights movement at the grassroots level.

The civil rights movement started in Maryland when the NAACP launched a legal attack on segregation. Charles Houston, with his prize former student

Howard Pindell in the early to mid-1930s. *Courtesy of Howard W. Pindell.*

Mid-Maryland: A Crossroads of History

Thurgood Marshall, sued the University of Maryland Law School in 1935. The law school had denied admission to Donald Murray solely on the basis of race. Moreover, no law school was available for black Marylanders. Judge Eugene O'Dunne ruled that Murray's rights to equal protection stipulated under the Fourteenth Amendment had been violated. He then ordered that the University of Maryland Law School be desegregated. The NAACP now had a tool—the law—with which to attack the system of Jim Crow itself, instead of simply responding to discrimination fostered by a segregated society.[1]

Ecstatic with the results, Houston ran off to other states to produce similar higher education rulings. In Missouri, Houston secured the *Missouri ex rel. Gaines v. Canada* decision. Lloyd Gaines had applied to the University of Missouri Law School and was denied because he was black. Gaines was given two choices: attend an out-of-state law school or apply to Lincoln University, the black university in Missouri, and the school would create a law school for blacks on demand. In 1938, the U.S. Supreme Court upheld the equal part of the "separate but equal" decision rendered in *Plessy v. Ferguson* in 1896: sending black students out of state or building a school on demand was not the same as attending the University of Missouri. The Supreme Court ruled that each state practicing segregation had to provide separate and equal law schools, and by implication separate and equal schools throughout the education system. Segregated education was going to become very expensive, and Houston had a national legal precedent to attack current practice.[2]

Meanwhile, Thurgood Marshall stayed in Maryland to work with the revitalized Baltimore Branch of the NAACP to develop new legal precedents in the education field at the primary and secondary levels. Marshall's first effort involved the public school system in Baltimore County. There were eleven white high schools and none for blacks. Marshall met with concerned citizens in Baltimore County who provided potential plaintiffs, raised funds and organized the NAACP branch for Baltimore County. Marshall found ample evidence that the school system was racially biased—textbooks, facilities, school terms and teachers' pay were all unequal. The most insidious practice was that black seventh graders had to take a test to determine if they qualified for admission to the black high school in Baltimore City. Only 50 percent ever passed the exam. If a student did pass the exam, then Baltimore County would pay four years' tuition through the eleventh grade. Black parents were responsible for transportation into the city or living arrangements for their children. White seventh graders did not take the test and rode county-provided school buses to county high schools. Unfortunately, Marshall lost his first solo civil rights case because he had chosen the wrong plaintiff. The young lady Marshall selected had completed the seventh grade twice and failed the exam twice. Hence, the judge ruled that she was not legally eligible for relief, despite the inequality that permeated the school system.[3]

Marshall's next task was to find a way to equalize teachers' salaries. According to state law, the minimum salaries of white teachers were nearly double those of black teachers. As illustrated in Table 1, the annual average salaries of Maryland county teachers reflected the legal intent of separate and unequal salaries—a position that Maryland was the only state to legally mandate.

Average Salaries of Maryland County Teachers, 1921–1939[4]

Year	Elementary Schools		High Schools	
	White	Colored	White	Colored
1921	$ 881	$ 442	$ 1,289	$ 864
1922	937	455	1,345	871
1923	990	513	1,436	906
1924	1,030	532	1,477	835
1925	1,057	546	1,485	808
1926	1,103	563	1,517	891
1927	1,126	586	1,534	908
1928	1,155	602	1,544	897
1929	1,184	621	1,557	879
1930	1,199	635	1,550	874
1931	1,217	643	1,559	882
1932	1,230	653	1,571	856
1933	1,231	657	1,532	837
1934	1,122	595	1,394	784
1935	1,135	602	1,398	790
1936	1,202	636	1,469	817
1937	1,220	653	1,488	821
1938	1,295	745	1,587	905
1939	1,314	848	1,595	991

Marshall found plenty of support for the idea of equalizing teachers' salaries. The Baltimore NAACP, led by Lillie Mae Jackson, teamed with the Maryland Educational Association (the black teachers' organization), headed by Enolia Pettigen, to form a joint committee to oversee the teachers' salary cases. The

Mid-Maryland: A Crossroads of History

Baltimore NAACP provided Marshall's legal services and the Maryland Educational Association agreed to cover the costs of the cases. It was clearly understood that if the teachers were going to profit from these cases, then they should supply the financing and plaintiffs. The association asked its members to each contribute five dollars to the joint committee and to join their local NAACP branch. To encourage teachers to risk their careers for this important cause, the joint committee agreed to pay one year's salary to any teacher who lost his or her job because of participation as a plaintiff in a case.[5]

The major concern was who would be the plaintiff. After the disastrous Baltimore County High School case, Marshall insisted on a teacher who supported the cause, had a solid record as an educator and was of good character. Enolia Pettigen thought of Howard Douglas Pindell. Born in 1908, Pindell was a native of Annapolis, Maryland. He had attended segregated schools in Anne Arundel County and Baltimore City, while working on a farm as a youth and in a variety of jobs during his teenage years. Hard work would be one of Pindell's trademarks. In a 1999 interview he noted, "I remember being so tired when I got home that when I got on my knees to say my prayers, I said, 'Our Father....' and when I got to 'Amen' it was morning."[6]

Pindell also worked hard in school, graduating from Douglas High School in 1927 and as class salutatorian from Morgan College in 1931. Pindell then took a job as a science teacher at Wiley H. Bates High School in Annapolis in the fall of 1931. He soon assumed various positions of leadership, serving as president of the Anne Arundel County Colored Teachers Association from 1932 to 1935 and president of the Annapolis Public Forum from 1933 to 1936. The Annapolis Public Forum met once a month "with the aim of creating an interest in civic affairs and of offering an outlet for the talent of the inhabitants of the community."[7] The forum met once a month and drew speakers from Baltimore and Washington, D.C., with only the collection plate offering for payment. Like its peer organization in Baltimore, the City-Wide Young People's Forum headed by Pindell's former high school classmate Juanita Jackson, the Annapolis Forum confronted the issue of race relations. Unlike the City-Wide Young People's Forum, however, the Annapolis Forum never became a civil rights organization.

As a young man, Pindell was aware of segregation and the places that black Americans could or could not go. But, he did not always heed the rules. Pindell noted, "I heard of these places, but I'm a daredevil. I would often go where you're not suppose to go and break down the barrier."[8] For example, Pindell commuted daily on the electric train between Baltimore and Annapolis. The last five seats in the back were reserved for blacks. If the seats were full, then blacks had to stand even if there were empty seats in the white section. Pindell made it a practice to sit in the last seat of the white section in order to make more room for other black passengers. His resistance proved successful because nobody ever confronted him.

When Enolia Pettigen of the Maryland Education Association approached Pindell about being a plaintiff, he was eager to do so. Pindell and Pettigen had worked together to try to get the Maryland legislature to change the law concerning segregated teacher salaries, but to no avail, and Pindell had long espoused desegregation of the schools. In a 1932 letter to the *Baltimore Afro-American* newspaper, Pindell argued that mixed schools were the only hope for real democracy.[9] He wrote Marshall in January 1936 and volunteered to be a plaintiff in the case for equal teachers' salaries. He was an ideal candidate. Pindell was in his fifth year of teaching, single and willing to engage in the struggle. "I am personally interested," he declared, "in seeing if this deplorable injustice can be removed by a fair and just decision of the courts in this State. Your capability as an attorney was concretely proven by your triumphant success in the University of Maryland case."[10]

Throughout the spring term, Marshall began preparing the case, and the white official in charge of black schools in Anne Arundel County began to shadow Pindell and hang around his classroom. In the summer of 1936, Pindell received an unexpected offer to be the principal of Lincoln High School in Frederick County, Maryland. Pindell asked Marshall for advice, knowing that accepting the job would scuttle the case Marshall had been preparing to challenge the unequal teachers' salaries. Marshall's response was, "Well, it's probably a kick upstairs but take it." Pindell took the promotion and headed to Frederick County.[11]

Marshall soon found another plaintiff in William Gibbs of Montgomery County. With the *Gibbs* case in 1937, Marshall got an out-of-court settlement after the Board of Education lost the preliminary court battles. Montgomery County agreed to equalize salaries over a two-year period. Teachers in other counties called Marshall to see if he could get their salaries equalized. Within months, nine of Maryland's twenty-three counties agreed to equalize teachers' salaries through out-of-court settlements.[12]

Meanwhile, Pindell was busy with his new job in Frederick County. He tackled a discipline problem, painted the building and restored stability to the school. "So when I went up to Frederick," Pindell remembered, "I took a low profile as far as teachers' salaries. I did organize the [county] teachers association…but I did not get involved in the salary situation. However, I think it followed me there."[13]

Mid-Maryland: A Crossroads of History

As Table 2 shows, teachers' salaries in Frederick County reflected the inequity found throughout the state.

Teachers' Salaries in Frederick County, 1935–1936[14]

	Elementary Schools		High Schools	
1935	White	Colored	White	Colored
Maryland	$1,135	602	1,398	790
Frederick	1,033	542	1,371	882
1936	White	Colored	White	Colored
Maryland	$1,202	636	1,469	817
Frederick	1,148	614	1,437	968

Thurgood Marshall and Dr. U.G. Bourne Sr., president of the Frederick NAACP, were both certainly interested in bringing the equal salaries struggle to Frederick County. Marshall called Judge Hammond Urner of Frederick County "one of the ablest and fairest judges in the State of Maryland."[15] Moreover, Judge Urner had ruled with the NAACP in the legal motion of the *Gibbs* case in Montgomery County. "Taking the entire matter into consideration," Marshall concluded, "I would say that Frederick County is one of the best counties in which to file one of these cases."[16]

Dr. Bourne agreed with Marshall's assessment, and convinced the Frederick NAACP to take up the issue of equal teachers' salaries in December 1937. Apparently, Bourne and/or other branch leaders approached the Frederick County Board of Education about equalizing the teachers' salaries because Bourne wrote back to Marshall saying, "We had reason to believe that this matter would be amicably adjusted, but at the last minute adequate provision has been denied us for the equalization of the teachers' salaries."[17]

Fed up with negotiation, Bourne was ready for a legal battle and offered to personally finance the case in Frederick County. The biggest problem, again, was finding a teacher to be the plaintiff. Bourne lamented that "no teacher seem[s] to have sufficient 'backbone' to contest the matter." The teachers feared losing their jobs, and Pindell had committed to attending summer school to earn his permanent principal's certificate. So, he would not be available for court appearances.

Bourne and the Frederick NAACP decided to continue their suit and formally petitioned the Board of Education in February 1938.[18] The petition, presented by Marshall and signed by nearly every black teacher in the county, noted the wage differentials between white and black teachers with identical qualifications, experience and duties, and that this differential on the basis of race was a violation of the equal protection laws guaranteed by the Fourteenth Amendment to the U.S. Constitution. The petition asked that the Board of Education "establish salary schedules for teachers and principals in Frederick County without distinction as to race or color of teacher or as to the school taught."[19]

The board responded by offering a 50 percent pay increase, but not equalization. The teachers now had a decision to make. They wavered back and forth until April, when Enolia Pettigen (now McMillan) addressed the teachers in Frederick County. Even with School Superintendent Eugene W. Pruitt in attendance, the teachers voted to press the Board of Education for a written response to their earlier petition. The thinking was that either the board would give in and equalize their salaries or the written response denying equal salaries would be used against the board in a future legal case.[20]

The board members, however, had no intention of equalizing salaries without a fight. In May 1938, the board approved a raise of $200 per year for black teachers, with principals and teachers who had earned advanced degrees getting another $50 per year. Although substantial, this salary increase was not the 50 percent that had been previously promised, and teachers would now have to work ten months instead of nine. Next, Superintendent Pruitt and the board turned on Howard Pindell, asking for his resignation on June 17, 1938. In a recent oral history interview, Pindell clearly recalled his feeling of shock and Pruitt's admonition, "don't ask me why!" Since coming to Frederick County, Pindell had effectively revitalized Lincoln High School, was ahead of schedule in his class work to secure his principal's certificate and believed he was in good standing with Pruitt and the Board of Education. Pindell refused to resign, so the board simply opted to not renew his contract. When Pindell had relocated from Anne Arundel County to Frederick County, he had lost his tenure. Moreover, the contract Pindell signed with Frederick County stipulated "that either of the parties to this contract may terminate it at the end of the first or second school year by giving thirty days' notice in writing to the other during the month of June or July." With no tenure and a clearly worded contract, discharging Pindell was a simple matter.[21]

The official reason given for Pindell's dismissal was that he was not qualified for the job. According to Pruitt, "When Mr. Pindell was appointed a qualified man was not available at the salary the Board of Education was able to pay. At the present time there are fully qualified men available, and we have an opportunity of getting them."[22] Hiring a person who already possessed a principal's certificate would immediately increase the percentage of certified

Mid-Maryland: A Crossroads of History

Howard Pindell, seated with 1938 graduates from Lincoln High School. *Courtesy of the Historical Society of Frederick County.*

teachers in Frederick County. True, Pindell had only a provisional principal's certificate, but he was ahead of the four-year schedule to obtain his full certification to which Pruitt and Pindell had verbally agreed in 1936. Plus, he now had two years of experience and was recognized, even by Pruitt, as having done an excellent job. In fact, the black residents cited his achievements when they protested his dismissal. Waiting one more year for Pindell to be fully qualified would have been reasonable.[23]

The real reason for Pindell's dismissal was probably to intimidate the other black teachers. First, Pindell was the leader of the black teachers in Frederick County. He was the highest-ranking teacher, as principal of Lincoln High School, and he was president of the Frederick County Colored Teachers Association. Second, although he had not volunteered to be the plaintiff, Pindell was considered to be one of the ringleaders in the salary fight in Frederick County. This may, in part, be due to the fact that Pindell was the first vice president of the Maryland Education Association, the organization which teamed with the NAACP to spearhead the salary equalization campaign. Moreover, Pindell had invited Enolia Pettigen McMillan to speak to the Frederick teachers twice in the spring of 1938. He was guilty by association, if nothing else. His letters with Mrs. McMillan certainly give the impression that he was quietly working with Dr. Bourne and the Frederick NAACP, of which he was a member, to press for equal teachers' salaries. In a subsequent memo to Walter White and Charles Houston, Thurgood Marshall noted that Pindell was "one of two teachers who have been leading the fight in Frederick County." More importantly, however, whites in Frederick believed Pindell was involved. An article in the Frederick newspaper stated, "He [Pindell] was active in the interests of his race at Annapolis and has continued this activity since coming here."[24]

Thurgood Marshall believed that Pindell was the victim of a conspiracy. "It is quite evident now," Marshall declared, "that there is a small bloc of County Superintendents who are definitely doing all in their power to defeat equalization of salaries. In this group we have Superintendent [Nicholas] Orem of Prince George's County, Superintendent E.W. Pruitt of Frederick County, and W. Stuart Fitzgerald of Somerset County. These superintendents have agreed to release as many colored teachers as possible in order to intimidate the other teachers."[25] In Pindell's case, according to Marshall, Pruitt had offered the principal position at Lincoln School, which was a promotion with a pay increase, even though Pindell did not have a principal's certificate. Pruitt had assured Pindell that he would be given a probationary certificate and would have four years to earn his permanent certificate. Unfortunately for Pindell, when he changed positions and county jurisdictions, he lost his tenure. Consequently, Frederick County could simply refuse to offer him a new contract after two years. "This is a roundabout way of putting a man out legally," Marshall concluded. Was Pindell the victim of duplicity as Marshall claimed? We will probably never know, although Pindell conceded it was possible.[26]

What is clear is that the idea of racial equality was not well received in Frederick County. In fact, despite the fact that Thurgood Marshall set a federal court precedent in Anne Arundel County in 1939 and the State of Maryland eliminated its separate and unequal salary schedule in 1941, Frederick County refused to equalize teachers' salaries until 1955. According to retired schoolteacher Bill Lee, it would not have happened even then except for a misrouted package. Lee was hired as the physical education teacher at Lincoln High School in August 1954. His pay was $2,700 per year. During the fall term that year, the wrong set of payroll checks was sent to Lincoln High. The office staff discovered that the checks for the white teachers were a different color and that the white teachers with comparable qualifications and experience were paid considerably more than the black teachers. After this discovery, and in light of the recent *Brown v. Board of Education* decision, the black teachers got a sudden pay raise in January 1955. Lee's salary, for example, jumped to $4,000 per year.[27] Frederick County did not equalize teachers' salaries until it felt compelled to do so. Thus, the struggle to secure equal teachers' salaries in Frederick County demonstrates that white resistance, sometimes subtle and legal, was also an integral part of the early civil rights movement.

The fight against segregated teachers' salaries in Frederick County also shows that the NAACP depended on strong grassroots support to implement its strategy. The NAACP could provide lawyers, armed with the Fourteenth Amendment, to create precedents that would undermine the legal status of segregation, but what they needed were individuals willing to serve as plaintiffs and black communities willing to support the cases financially and otherwise. Frederick County had the latter, with a local NAACP branch organized, promise of financial support from Dr. U.G. Bourne Sr. and a judge deemed friendly to the NAACP's legal argument.

Nonetheless, the very real fear of reprisal, as displayed in the dismissal of Howard Pindell, paralyzed the black teachers and kept them from coming forward as plaintiffs. Frederick Douglass once said, "Power concedes nothing without a demand. It never did and it never will." The black teachers of Frederick County had been willing to ask for a raise but were unwilling to demand the end of segregated salaries. In short, the combination of white resistance and black reluctance stalled the early civil rights movement in Frederick County.

Bibliography

Baltimore Afro-American. Select dates, 1932–38.

Frederick County. *Annual Report of the Auditors of Frederick County, Maryland*, 1954–55. Special Collections, University of Maryland at College Park.

Journal of Proceedings. Board of Education of Frederick County. June 8, 1938. Frederick County Public Schools, Hayward Road Complex, Frederick, MD.

African American History

Lee, William O. Interview with author. August 15, 2000.

McNeil, Genna Rae. *Groundwork: Charles Hamilton Houston and the Struggle for Civil Rights*. Philadelphia: University of Pennsylvania Press, 1983.

NAACP Papers. Library of Congress, Washington, D.C.

Orser, W. Edward. "Neither Separate Nor Equal: Foreshadowing *Brown* in Baltimore County, 1935–1937." *Maryland Historical Magazine* 92 (Spring 1997): 5–35.

Pindell, Howard D. Interview by Jenni Hess, November 18, 1999. OH 069, Oral History Collection, Frederick Community College, Frederick, MD.

———. Papers. Catoctin Center for Regional Studies, Frederick Community College, Frederick, MD.

Thompson, Bruce A. "The Civil Rights Vanguard: The NAACP and the Black Community in Baltimore, 1931–1942." PhD diss., University of Maryland at College Park, 1996.

Tushnet, Mark V. *The NAACP Legal Strategy against Segregated Education, 1925–1950*. Chapel Hill: University of North Carolina Press, 1987.

Civil War Era

Mid-Maryland's role in the Civil War proved important in several respects. First, as the most northern of the southern states, and the state that borders the nation's capital on three sides, Maryland exhibited a pronounced ambiguity at the outbreak of the war.[1] As a border state, Maryland witnessed "brother fighting brother." And due to Maryland's location, Lincoln could not afford to have the Old Line State join the new Confederacy.

Secondly, western Maryland provided the logical gateway for any Confederate invasion of the North. With the Potomac River as the only major geographical obstacle, and with the mountains to shield their movements, the Confederates took advantage of the terrain in both of their forays north of the Potomac. Lastly, the area produced soldiers and officers for both the North and the South, as well as civilians willing to make significant sacrifices as the armies moved through the area and fought engagements.

Jessica Cannon, a Frederick Community College graduate now in the history doctoral program at Rice University, investigates the support of Henry David Thoreau, a noted pacifist, for John Brown after his raid on Harpers Ferry, Virginia. After briefly recounting the events of October 16–18, 1859, Cannon examines a number of Thoreau's writings, including his "Plea for Captain John Brown," which provided a justification and even vindication of Brown's actions in attempting to foment an insurrection. A pattern emerges, according to Cannon, in which Thoreau's pacifism is not unlimited; violence, in fact, is justifiable in the pursuit of upholding the sanctity of natural law over unjust civil law so long as one is willing to be held accountable for one's actions.

Mid-Maryland: A Crossroads of History

Michael Powell, professor of history at Frederick Community College, re-examines an issue that was long thought resolved: that Frederick County, while divided in its sympathies, was decidedly pro-Northern. This is not the case, according to Powell's contribution. By relying primarily upon newspapers and election returns, Powell uses the presidential election of 1860 to prove that Frederick County immediately prior to the secession crisis was, in fact, Southern in its interests and the voters cast their ballots to protect those interests. Both John Breckinridge and John Bell were presented as candidates who would protect the Southerners' rights, as opposed to Abraham Lincoln who was viewed as a divisive sectional candidate. The county voted overwhelmingly for the two "Southern" candidates, with Bell winning by a scant majority. Ironically, the voting pattern in Frederick County was different from that in other parts of the South. In Frederick County, John Breckinridge, the most ardent Southern candidate, captured the election districts with both the highest percentage of slavery and those with among the lowest. Not only is this contrary to voting patterns in the rest of the South, but it also raises significant questions regarding the correlation between slave-holding and voting patterns in the upper South.

Brian Baracz, a Frederick Community College graduate and student at the University of Maryland Baltimore County, presents an overview of the military career of Bradley Tyler Johnson, a long-neglected subject worthy of serious inquiry. This Confederate general, born and raised in Frederick, practiced law and was the state's attorney for Frederick County prior to the war. As Baracz shows, Johnson was instrumental in raising and commanding troops from Maryland for the Confederacy. While leading the Marylanders, he faced conflicts both within the ranks and with his fellow officers, particularly General John McCausland. But none of this diminished Johnson's role as a leader or his troops' triumphs at the battles of Front Royal, Harrisonburg (Virginia), and Second Manassas (Bull Run). Finishing his military career as commander of the Confederate prison at Salisbury, North Carolina, Johnson was a tireless supporter of the "Lost Cause" after the war.

The remaining two articles of this section address a significant issue inherent to any war: the impact of the fighting on civilians who lived near the battlefields. Edith Wallace, a historian with Paula Reed & Associates, relies heavily upon the private letters of the Jacob Miller family as well as government documents in assessing the effects of the battle of Antietam on the residents of Sharpsburg. The residents' first concern was safety for themselves and their families, but it was after the battle that the devastation could be most keenly felt. Bodies of soldiers and animals littering the battlefield, crops and farm animals destroyed, homes frequently damaged or in ruins, sick and wounded soldiers needing medical attention—these were some of the overwhelming problems faced by the citizens of Sharpsburg after the September 17, 1862 battle. Through the experiences of some Sharpsburg residents, Wallace is able to bring a personal perspective of the devastation wrought by these military engagements.

Kari Turner, a graduate of both Frederick Community College and Mount St. Mary's College who is currently pursuing a master's degree in history at the University of Maryland, examines the role of Frederick's citizens in caring for the sick and wounded during the course of the war. While many of the studies in this area are focused on military and political events, Turner's contribution draws our attention to a subject heretofore largely ignored in the history of central Maryland. As Turner notes, Frederick housed General Hospital Number One for the Union army, and throughout the war, the sick and wounded were cared for in Frederick. After the larger engagements in the area, such as Gettysburg, Monocacy and Antietam, Frederick became overwhelmed with the wounded from both sides. Turner notes the medical assistance received by the soldiers, but her real focus is the care extended by the citizens of Frederick beyond that of medical assistance: writing letters for soldiers, providing clothing, food, or comfort in prayer and a host of other kindnesses.

Thoreau and His American Hero:

In Support of John Brown's "Raid"

Jessica A. Cannon

The events that transpired on October 16, 17 and 18, 1859, at Harpers Ferry, Virginia, weighed heavily upon the public prior to, and at the outset of, the American Civil War.[1] Initially, John Brown's insurrection[2] sparked vehement and opposing reactions in the North and South, as incomplete and exaggerated details filtered out to national newspapers. Some viewed Brown as a brutal murderer, revolutionary enemy and extremist fanatic who, at the least, had temporarily lost control of his mental faculties, and at most, was clinically insane. Abolitionists and anti-slavery followers tended to view Brown in a more heroic light and after his death saw him to be a martyr for the anti-slavery cause. Many citizens in the South viewed his actions and ideas as a threat to their economic institution and personal safety; many in the North viewed him as a devout and righteous man who acted on his principles over the laws and the Constitution, for better or worse.

Many prominent Northern public figures—Ralph Waldo Emerson, Henry Ward Beecher, Wendell Phillips and Henry David Thoreau, for instance—

Photo of Harpers Ferry, circa 1862. *Courtesy of the Harpers Ferry National Historic Park, National Park Service.*

Mid-Maryland: A Crossroads of History

spoke out in defense of John Brown. Yet it was Thoreau's defense of John Brown that was most surprising. Despite being an advocate of non-violence and passive resistance, Thoreau wrote and delivered the speech "A Plea for Captain John Brown" in support of Brown's truculent insurrection at Harpers Ferry. The transcendentalist author supported neither immediate abolitionism nor slavery, so his outspoken opinion defending Brown's ideals and actions seems paradoxical. Thoreau respected Brown for his righteous spirit and abolitionist beliefs, his resolute dedication to the anti-slavery cause, his self-sacrificial methods to evoke change and his determination to uphold justice and natural law over the injustices in civil law that had evolved from sectional politics and corrupt government. And, this respect was deep enough to override his own pacifism. In essence, John Brown became a hero to Thoreau.

The road to Harpers Ferry was a long and circuitous path that began in Brown's youth. John Brown was born May 9, 1800, in Torrington, Connecticut. From his earliest days, Brown was raised with staunch religious and hardworking family values. These strong religious values and his father's admonition "to view the enslavement of Negroes as a sin against God" had a lasting influence on Brown for the remainder of his life.[3]

Another significant event in Brown's life was his mother's death when he was eight. Brown's father soon remarried, but Brown showed no affection for his stepmother and "was thus left without any tempering influence on his diffident but haughty and self-reliant nature."[4] During this time in Brown's childhood, he was not concerned with an education and, instead, aided his father in business endeavors. One business venture required young Brown to drive cattle for his father, who supplied beef to troops in Michigan during the War of 1812. On that trip he noticed a particular landlord gentleman's slave boy, who was around his age. The boy was "badly clothed, poorly fed…& beaten before his [John's] eyes with…any other thing that first came to hand." Enraged, "John returned home 'a most determined Abolitionist' swearing 'Eternal war with Slavery.'"[5] This event sparked an ardent passion that would ennoble Brown to further action against slavery later in life.

With the passage of the Kansas-Nebraska Act in 1854, which produced violent clashes between the pro-slavery and anti-slavery forces in the territories, Brown moved to Kansas at the request of several of his sons, who had gone there earlier in the decade to defend the anti-slavery cause After pro-slavery forces attacked the town of Lawrence in May of 1856, Brown, "proclaiming himself an instrument of God's will," attacked five unarmed pro-slavery men and brutally murdered them along the banks of the Pottawatomie Creek. The Pottawatomie Creek Massacre, as the incident came to be known, along with other violent guerrilla attacks made by Brown and his men, gained them national press. This name recognition soon aided Brown in raising financial support and supplies for his other endeavors amongst the abolitionists in New England.[6]

Brown's next notable actions involved organizing his supporters and finalizing his plans for the attack against slavery; he then would move his operations to the Blue Ridge Mountains. In 1858 at a "Constitutional Convention" held in Canada, Brown, his followers and his Northern financiers outlined the objectives of Brown's plan to attack the institution of slavery. His primary objective would be to attack the practice in the South by arming the slaves, thus intimidating white Southerners. He then would move into the Blue Ridge Mountains, creating a stronghold for himself and the slaves who would join his cause. According to one historian, Brown "was organizing a forcible attack on slavery, because without question he held the conviction that slavery was an organized menace to the existence of the American Republic."[7]

There are different historiographical interpretations of Brown's plan and the reasons for the attack on Harpers Ferry, but it is clear John Brown was "a leader of men and a born strategist," as well as "a student of warfare." Brown "had studied the census, and knew the resources of the region in which he designed to operate."[8] Although Brown's reasons for selecting Harpers Ferry were not recorded, possible reasons range from Brown's intentions of being caught in order to become a martyr for the anti-slavery cause (since Harpers Ferry lies below three mountain cliffs and is virtually indefensible), to Harpers Ferry's readily accessible arsenal and proximity to the Blue Ridge Mountains, the expected area of retreat for the concentration of Brown's forces and a later, larger attack on slavery. However, if Brown were attempting to eliminate slavery and free large numbers of slaves, he selected the wrong location. The Kennedy Farmhouse, Brown's base of operations, was located in Washington County, Maryland. Washington County had only 1,435 slaves, with a total white population of 28,305. Furthermore, the Maryland election districts near Harpers Ferry and containing the communities of Boonsboro, Sandy Hook, Pleasant Valley and Sharpsburg had a total of only 453 slaves.[9] This region was not home to thousands of slaves who could have readily joined Brown's cause. Harpers Ferry was only practical if Brown quickly seized the weapons at the arsenal and retreated the same night.

After selecting his location and organizing the plan, Brown enlisted additional financial support and men, and by spring of 1859 had moved a major portion of his supplies and "soldiers" to the Kennedy Farmhouse in Maryland. On the night of Sunday, October 16, 1859, John Brown and his

Mid-Maryland: A Crossroads of History

John Brown before October 1859. *Courtesy of the Harpers Ferry National Historic Park, National Park Service.*

eighteen men of the "Provisional Army" began their attack. Armed with pikes and rifles, they made their way from the Kennedy Farmhouse to the covered railroad bridge that joined Maryland Heights to Harpers Ferry. After capturing the bridge, the small army proceeded to the armory yard along the Potomac bank and took control of the armory. That night Brown's men gathered prisoners from the town, including Colonel Lewis Washington, a great-grandnephew of George Washington who possessed a sword that had belonged to General Washington, which Brown desired to have for symbolic purposes. All of the prisoners were brought to the watch house and Brown's men spent the night in the armory yard. In the course of the night and the early morning hours, word spread that Brown had taken hostages and was ensconced in the armory.[10]

The following day brought little activity until noon. John Brown had stationed his men at several locations—the bridge, armory and rifle works—and by midmorning these men were under gunfire by the townspeople. However, the townspeople were not organized and had few guns, thus doing little damage. Later in the day, other organized militia from surrounding communities arrived by train. They pinned Brown and his remaining men and hostages in the engine house, but were unable to rescue the hostages, due to fierce gunfire.[11] Troops continued to arrive from Winchester, Frederick, and Shepherdstown, but no more active engagements took place that day. Late that night a detachment of marines from the Washington Navy Yard arrived under the immediate command of Lieutenant Israel Green, but led by Colonel Robert E. Lee. By the morning of the eighteenth, the marines were in position surrounding the engine house. At dawn, Lee made an offer to John Brown for his surrender, but Brown refused. Soon thereafter, with Lieutenant Green in the lead, the Federal troops stormed the engine house, and after battering the heavy wooden doors open, the marines rushed Brown's men, killing or capturing them. The attack took only a matter of minutes, and no hostages were injured. Brown, however, had been struck multiple times by Lieutenant Green's sword and suffered head and neck wounds.[12]

John Brown and his four surviving soldiers were taken to the jail in Charles Town, Virginia (now West Virginia). They were arraigned on October 25, 1859, and indicted the next day for treason against the Commonwealth of Virginia, conspiring with slaves to rebel, and murder. Brown was tried first, with his trial beginning on October 27 and lasting four days. Still suffering from his wounds, he had to lie on a cot for the trial. On October 31 the court found him guilty on all three charges; he was sentenced to death on November 2.

During the interim weeks between Brown's trial and execution, martial law was declared in Charles Town and militiamen patrolled the town and surrounding countryside to prevent further uprisings or interference from citizens. At approximately 11:00 a.m. on the morning of December 2, 1859, Brown was led to a field just outside town. Fifteen hundred soldiers surrounded the field, and no civilians were permitted near the execution site. At 11:30 a.m. John Brown died.[13]

Brown had hoped that his insurrection would inspire the local slaves to join him and aid in a rebellion against the slave owners who he felt corrupted both the national government and society. It is clear that Brown intended to be violent and did carry out his actions in a violent manner. From the initial planning stages, Brown planned to arm the slaves and provoke an uprising. Yet, despite the knowledge of Brown's actions in Kansas and his violence at Harpers Ferry, Henry David Thoreau, a champion of passive resistance and non-violent civil disobedience, believed in and defended Brown for his principles and actions. Thoreau, an advocate for the abolition of slavery on the basis of morality and higher law, wrote about the rights of the citizen to reign in or change the government. Thoreau's respect for Brown's belief in the superiority of natural laws over Constitutional and human laws is illustrated in several journal entries: "He [Brown] was a superior man. He did not value his bodily life in comparison with ideal things; he did not recognize unjust human laws, but resisted them as he was bid."[14] Brown did not follow the Constitution and earthly laws that forbade assisting slaves to rebel or escape and that forbade armed insurrection against the government, as the Commonwealth of Virginia claimed when Brown was charged with treason. Brown instead believed in the equality of all men and fought to uphold this as a natural law ideal. Continuing later in his journal, Thoreau wrote of Brown, "Our thoughts could not revert to any greater or wiser or better men with whom to compare him, for he was above them all. The man this country was about to hang was the greatest and best in it."[15]

Mid-Maryland: A Crossroads of History

To Thoreau, Brown's most endearing quality was his righteousness. In a speech entitled "A Plea for Captain John Brown," Thoreau said of Brown, "A man of rare common sense and directness of speech, as of action; a transcendentalist above all, a man of ideas and principles, that was what distinguished him. Not yielding to a whim or transient impulse, but carrying out the purpose of a life."[16] In short, Thoreau held John Brown in the highest esteem as a hero for the enslaved man and for the country. Ralph Waldo Emerson, a mentor and friend of Thoreau, echoed Thoreau in praising Brown in a speech he delivered at a relief meeting for the Brown family in November of 1859. "Indeed, it is the *reductio ad absurdum* of Slavery, when the Governor of Virginia is forced to hang a man whom he declares to be a man of the most integrity, truthfulness, and courage he has ever met."[17]

In addition to Brown's righteous vindication of natural law, Thoreau was in awe of the dedication and self-sacrifices Brown and his family made for the abolitionist cause. As Thoreau wrote, "When I consider the spectacle of himself, and his six sons, and his son-in-law, enlisted for this fight, proceeding coolly, reverently, humanely to work, while almost all Americans stood ranked on the other side, I say again that it effects me as a sublime spectacle."[18] At Harpers Ferry, John Brown, determined to continue, saw one of his sons shot to death under a flag of truce and another slowly bleed to death in the night.[19] Despite his personal losses, Brown still persisted in his endeavors. John Brown viewed his life, and ultimately the lives of his family and followers, as subservient to the greater cause for the abolition of slavery. Note Brown's words to his children in a letter dated "Akron 8th May 1846," in which he wrote, "I am always glad to learn that my family are in health, but more glad to learn they are doing right."[20] Clearly, Brown's first priority was to do right and fight the good fight for the cause; personal risks and welfare were not as important as were ideals and goals.

Thoreau expressed "that government is best that governs least" in his essay "Civil Disobedience." Deriving his ideas on the rights and responsibilities of citizens from the Declaration of Independence, Thoreau wrote, "I think that we should be men first and subjects afterward." Therefore, according to Thoreau, one had to be an individual before one could be a participant in the government; each individual citizen had to discover his or her own ethical principles, intuitions and thought processes before those individuals could understand their desires in a government or create a moral and sound government founded in natural law. "Let every man," Thoreau stated, "make known what kind of government would command his respect, and that will be one step toward obtaining it." Hence, society had a moral obligation

Civil War Era

Henry David Thoreau in 1856. *Courtesy of the Henry David Thoreau Society, www.thoreausociety.org.*

before it had a political obligation; the government, as an extension of the ethical and moral voting society, had to uphold natural laws that were morally right over unjust civil laws. Thoreau wrote on the concept; Brown acted on it.[21]

In Thoreau's view, the government was not upholding these morals and therefore he would no longer support the government: "I cannot for an instant recognize that political organization as my government which is the slave's government also." Thoreau, like the founding forefathers stated in the Declaration of Independence, believed that when the government overstepped its powers and imposed upon its citizens unjustly, those citizens ultimately had a right to revolution. In "Civil Disobedience," Thoreau wrote, "All men recognize the right of revolution; that is, the right to refuse allegiance to, and to resist, the government, when its tyranny or its inefficiency are great and unendurable." According to Thoreau, "Unjust laws exist: shall we be content to obey them, or shall we endeavor to amend them, and obey them until we have succeeded or shall we transgress them at once?" Thoreau also identified three ways to react to unjust laws; citizens can choose to do nothing about the unjust law, they can choose to work through the system to change the law in due time, or they can choose to break the law. Thoreau added that if a law "is of such a nature that it requires you to be the agent of injustice to another, then, I say, break the law."[22]

Following Thoreau's logic, Brown chose one of his options as a citizen, and transgressed the law in order to bring about change in a system that violated the natural laws by holding a race in bondage and not in equality. However, Thoreau also states in "Civil Disobedience" that a citizen who chooses to transgress or break the civil law understands and must be willing to accept civil punishment. It is abundantly clear that Brown was willing to accept his penalty when he fought to the death with soldiers and townsmen in Harpers Ferry, or

Mid-Maryland: A Crossroads of History

when he courageously approached the gallows without any reservation. To the Virginia court, and obviously the nation beyond, Brown stated, "Now, if it is deemed necessary that I should forfeit my life for the furtherance of the ends of justice, and mingle my blood with the blood of millions in this slave country whose rights are disregarded by wicked, cruel, and unjust enactments, I say let it be done."[23] Brown clearly understood and accepted his civil punishment.

Some people consider Brown's actions revolutionary and illegal. He was attempting to cause slaves to rise in rebellion against their masters and the American government, and he committed numerous crimes, among them murder, theft, treason and kidnapping. Yet, Thoreau justified this disobedience as a legitimate option for reformation in a government that was corrupt for not advocating an end to slavery. In commenting on Brown's insurrection and its relation to the current political situation, Thoreau noted, "I regard this event as a touchstone designed to bring out with glaring distinctiveness the character of this government."[24] This belief that the government was overstepping its boundaries was reiterated in "A Plea for Captain John Brown" when Thoreau spoke of the insurrection. Brown "had the courage to face his country herself when she was in the wrong."[25] His actions against the Commonwealth of Virginia, and his attempt to promote a general rebellion to achieve freedom for the slave populations across the United States, were necessary actions. As author William Elsey Connelley wrote in language reminiscent of Thoreau, "Virginia was compelled to hang John Brown to preserve slavery, but his death did more to forward universal emancipation than his life could ever have accomplished had he had all the successes he hoped for."[26]

Thoreau wrote "A Plea for Captain John Brown" neither to defend Brown as a fallible man nor to save him from the sentence of death, but to preserve the soul of the man Thoreau himself admired for his principles. "I know that there have been a few heroes in the land, but no man has ever stood up in America for the dignity of human nature so devotedly, persistently, and so effectively as this man."[27] This speech was about John Brown the ideal and his principles, not the man. Thoreau wanted the public to see Brown not as an insane murderer, but as a revolutionary and martyr for the cause of freedom, similar to the revolutionary forefathers: "He was like the best of those who stood at Concord Bridge once, on Lexington Common, and on Bunker Hill, only he was firmer and higher principled than any that I have chanced to hear of as there."[28] Brown, according to Thoreau, would be remembered as a hero and a model of righteous citizenship. Speaking of Brown and his soldiers, Thoreau said, "These men, in teaching us how to die, have at the same time taught us how to live."[29]

Civil War Era

Thoreau's journal entry dated October 21, 1859, recapitulates his defense of John Brown perfectly: "I do not complain of any tactics that are effective of good, whether one wields the quill or the sword, but I shall not think him mistaken who quickest succeeds to liberate the slave. I will judge of the tactics by the fruits."[30]

Thoreau was unable to attend the memorial service held for John Brown on July 4, 1860, in North Elba, New York, but expressed his thoughts in "The Last Days of John Brown," a speech he wrote for the service that was later published in *The Liberator*. His conclusion summates the ideal of John Brown and what Brown exemplified in life and in death:

> *On the day of his translation, I heard, to be sure, that he was hung, but I did not know what that meant; I felt no sorrow on that account; but not for a day or two did I even hear that he was dead, and not after any number of days shall I believe it. Of all the men who were said to be my contemporaries, it seemed to me that John Brown was the only one who had not died. I never hear of a man named Brown now—and I hear of them pretty often,—I never hear of any particularly brave and earnest man, but my first thought is of John Brown, and what relation he may be to him. I meet him at every turn. He is more alive than ever he was. He has earned immortality. He is no longer confined to North Elba nor to Kansas. He is no longer working in secret. He works in public, and in the clearest light that shines on this land.*"[31]

It is clear that Thoreau saw the spirit of John Brown and his principles alive and well around him in life. Even if Brown the person were dead, the ideal of John Brown lived on in the hearts of reformers.

In conclusion, despite the non-violent tendencies of Henry David Thoreau, he supported a brutal and violent reformer in John Brown. He supported the man for his ideals and principles, overlooking Brown's flaws as a fallible man. Thoreau respected Brown for his righteous spirit, his dedication to the abolition of slavery and to reform, his self-sacrificial methods and his determination to uphold justice and natural law over the injustices in civil law that had devolved from politics and a corrupt government. Thoreau did not condone violence as a general rule, but, as he stated in "Civil Disobedience," there are times when it becomes necessary to change a corrupt government, and it is a civic duty to take the necessary actions—violent or not—to effectuate that change.

MID-MARYLAND: A Crossroads of History

Bibliography

Brown, John, Akron, Ohio, to [his children], ALS, 8 May 1846. Harpers Ferry Document 75. Harpers Ferry Archives, Harpers Ferry National Historic Park Library and Archives, Harpers Ferry, WV.

Connelley, William Elsey. *John Brown*. Topeka, KS: Crane & Company, 1900.

1860 Federal Census Collection. Collection no. MSA SC 4335, film M7230. Maryland State Archives, Hall of Records, Annapolis.

Hinton, Richard J. *John Brown and His Men*. New York: Funk & Wagnalls Co., 1894. Reprint, New York: Arno Press, Inc., 1968.

Kennedy, Joseph C.G. *Population of the United States in 1860; Compiled from the Original Census Under the Direction of the Secretary of the Interior*. Washington, D.C.: Government Printing Office, 1864. Reprint, New York: Norman Ross Publishing Inc., 1990.

National Park Service, Department of the Interior. *John Brown's Raid*. Washington, D.C.: Government Printing Office, 1990.

Oates, Stephen B. *To Purge This Land With Blood: A Biography of John Brown*. New York: Harper & Row, 1970.

Redpath, James. *Echoes of Harper's Ferry*. Boston: Thayer and Eldridge, 1860. Reprint, Westport, CT: Negro Universities Press, 1970.

Richardson Jr., Robert D. *Henry Thoreau: A Life of the Mind*. Berkley, CA: University of California Press, 1986.

Thoreau, Henry David. "Civil Disobedience." In *Walden and Other Writings of Henry David Thoreau*, edited by Brooks Atkinson. The Modern Library Edition. New York: Random House, 1992.

———. *The Journals of Henry David Thoreau*, edited by Bradford Torrey and Francis H. Allen. Vol. 2. New York: Dover Publications, Inc., 1962.

———. "The Last Days of John Brown." In *The Portable Thoreau*, edited by Carl Bode. The Viking Portable Library Edition. New York: Penguin Books, 1982.

———. "A Plea for Captain John Brown." In *Walden and Other Writings of Henry David Thoreau*, edited by Brooks Atkinson. The Modern Library Edition. New York: Random House, 1992.

Warren, Robert Penn. *John Brown: The Making of a Martyr*. Nashville, TN: J.S. Sanders & Company, 1993.

"With Her Southern Sisters":

Frederick County and the Election of 1860

Michael A. Powell

Those familiar with Frederick County history in the Civil War era know the story of the presidential election of 1860. It tells us that the results of the election reflected the divisiveness of the county and yet did not demonstrate support for the Southern cause. According to this interpretation, while there was certainly Southern sentiment in the county, as a whole the county strongly supported the Union and its cause.[1] Yet a close examination of the election reveals a different story. It shows that Frederick County, in fact, was very strong in its Southern sympathies, identified its interests with the South and sought, through the electoral process, the candidates most likely to protect those interests.

By the spring of 1860, national politics was in disarray. In the forefront of discussion were the questions of states' rights and the extension of slavery in

Political cartoon parodying candidates in the 1860 election. Lincoln and Douglas (to the left) are tearing at the West, while Breckinridge (center) rips the South away from the rest of the country. Bell (to the right) stands on a stool trying to glue the nation together. *Courtesy of the Library of Congress.*

Mid-Maryland: A Crossroads of History

the territories. The nation was still smarting from John Brown's raid in Harpers Ferry in October 1859. The House of Representatives was deadlocked along sectional lines during December and January over the election of the Speaker of the House. Only on the forty-fourth ballot would the bland William Pennington of New Jersey be grudgingly elected. The Congress of the United States, due to the open hostility between Northerners and Southerners, had become an armed camp; as noted by one senator, "the only persons who do not have a revolver and knife are those who have two revolvers."[2]

The stage was set for national conventions, beginning in April 1860 with the Democratic Party. The Democratic National Convention met on April 23 in Charleston, South Carolina. Stephen Douglas, author of popular sovereignty and the politician who was able to push through the Compromise of 1850, had long coveted the presidency. When he arrived in Charleston, Douglas expected to receive the nomination, but he fell short of the required two-thirds majority. The Southern Democrats then insisted on a platform including federal protection of slavery in the territories, which of course ran counter to Douglas's position on popular sovereignty. Douglas won this platform battle, but his victory prompted Southern delegates to walk out of the convention. Since Douglas could not command the votes of even two-thirds of the remaining delegates (much less two-thirds of all Democratic delegates), the convention adjourned, agreeing to reconvene in Baltimore on June 18. As Jacob Engelbrecht of Frederick aptly observed, "The Democrat Convention Met at Charleston, S.C.-April 23, 1860, but could not agree, too much North & too much South."[3]

In Baltimore, yet again, the Southern contingent wanted a plank in the platform guaranteeing their interest in slavery, but Douglas would not commit to such. After a number of Southern state delegates were denied admission to the Baltimore convention because of their insistence of a pro-slavery plank in the party's platform, the Southern states, including half of the Maryland delegation, bolted to attend a convention of their own. While Douglas received the nomination of the first convention, John C. Breckinridge of Kentucky was selected by the Southern Democrats as their presidential candidate. Both factions' platforms supported the "acquisition of Cuba…at the earliest practicable moment, the faithful execution of the Fugitive Slave Law" and "construction of a Railroad to the Pacific coast, at the earliest practicable period." With the Democratic Party committed to national expansion, governmental protection of slavery in the territories assumed critical importance. As historian Arthur Bestor observes, this authority over territories during expansion was "the narrow channel through which surged the torrent of ideas and interests and anxieties that flooded down from every drenched hillside upon which the storm cloud of slavery discharged its poisoned rain."[4]

The disagreement that divided the Democratic Party centered on slavery in the territories and, specifically, to what extent the federal government should protect the slaveholders' interest. The Douglas Democrats' platform stated that "the Democratic Party will abide by the decision of the Supreme Court of the United States, over the institution of slavery within the Territories."[5] Certainly, to Southerners, this was no guarantee of slavery; not only could the Supreme Court revisit the slavery issue and change or modify its *Dred Scott* decision, but Douglas also articulated his belief that popular sovereignty did not conflict with *Dred Scott* and was consistent with the Supreme Court! The Breckinridge Democratic plank on slavery created a positive responsibility of the federal government in protecting and defending "the rights of persons and property in the Territories, and wherever else its constitutional authority extends."[6]

As divided and disarrayed as were the Democrats, the Republicans were unified and confident. The Republican convention, beginning on May 16 in Chicago, obviously selected Abraham Lincoln from Illinois. But Lincoln was not the party's first choice. William H. Seward of New York went into the convention as the most well-known and respected Republican of the time. But he had earned the enmity of other Republican factions over the years and was perceived as being extremely radical with respect to slavery. As the originator of the term "irrepressible conflict" in describing the North/South confrontation, Seward had stated in 1858:

> *Shall I tell you what this collision means? They who think that it is accidental, unnecessary work of interested or fanatical agitators, and therefore ephemeral mistake the case altogether. It is an irrepressible conflict between opposing and enduring forces; it means that the United States must and will, sooner or later, become entirely a slaveholding nation, or entirely a free labor nation.*[7]

Lincoln, on the other hand, offered much to the party. He was from Illinois, a key state that the Republicans had to win if they expected victory in 1860. He also was an experienced politician who earned his reputation as an antislavery advocate in his debates with Stephen Douglas in 1858 when both were running for an Illinois Senate seat. At the same time, it was well known in the North that Lincoln deplored the extreme abolitionist position with respect to slavery and argued not for elimination of slavery, but rather for no further extension of the peculiar institution into the territories. Lastly, Lincoln was characterized by the "Honest Abe" image, which certainly would not hurt. With these attributes, Lincoln captured the nomination on the third ballot.

Harkening to the Declaration of Independence and its reliance on natural law, the Republican platform condemned the extension of slavery into the territories as "subversive of the peace and harmony of the country." And in direct confrontation with both factions of the Democratic Party, the platform asserted "that the normal condition of all territory of the United States is that of freedom…[and] it becomes our duty, by legislation, whenever such legislation is necessary, to maintain this provision of the Constitution [the Fifth Amendment regarding due process of law] against all attempts to violate it; and we deny the authority of Congress, of a territorial legislature, or any individuals to give legal existence to slavery in any territory of the United States." The platform also supported protective tariffs, a homestead act to encourage settlement of the western lands and a railroad to the Pacific Ocean.[8]

A new, third party made its first appearance in the national election of 1860. John J. Crittenden of Kentucky, acknowledged as a leading moderate of the day, believed that neither the Democrats nor Republicans had the interests of the Union at heart; both were too intractable over the slavery issue. Crittenden was instrumental in creating the Constitutional Union Party, whose slogan was "The Union, the Constitution, and the Enforcement of the Laws;" yet the congressman from Kentucky declined to accept the presidential nomination if it were offered. With the nomination wide open, John Bell, a slaveholder from Tennessee, edged out Sam Houston of Texas. The platform reflected the goal of the party to avoid the sectional conflict and adopt a general, non-sectionally harmonious statement: "it is the part of patriotism and of duty to *recognize* no political principle other than THE CONSTITUTION OF THE COUNTRY, THE UNION OF THE STATES, AND THE ENFORCEMENT OF THE LAWS…we hereby pledge ourselves to maintain, protect, and defend, separately and unitedly this great principle of public liberty and national safety against all enemies, at home and abroad."[9]

With the candidates for the 1860 election selected by the parties, much of the electioneering occurred at the local level. An examination of the evidence available to historians gives us a glimpse of how this national election played out in Frederick County. This county is both blessed and cursed when studying the Civil War era: there exists a fabulously rich diary written by Jacob Engelbrecht, as well as diaries by Catherine Markell and Margaret Scholl

Hood. Researchers of the election of 1860 quite rightly have relied heavily on Mr. Engelbrecht's accounts, for his diary is full of detail and imagery. Yet, Mr. Engelbrecht, who lived across the street from Barbara Fritchie on West Patrick Street, was unabashedly and decidedly pro-Union.[10] And therein lies the curse. To rely upon his diary exclusively means to accept a pro-Union perspective on an extremely sensitive issue with decidedly far-reaching implications. Mrs. Markell, who was decidedly pro-Southern, wrote a diary that is uneven for the historian; at times she provides insightful perceptions and vivid descriptions, at other times she offers a wealth of information about who visited whom. Margaret Hood's diary allows the reader a glimpse into the life of a relatively well-to-do young lady who visits and shops. Therefore, these last two diaries offer little for historians with respect to this election.

The other major source of information for this period is the press. As one historian has observed, the newspaper was "the primary source of information for the general public in 1860." Therefore, the study of the newspapers at that time should yield significant insights. However, the papers were not impartial; editors were "essentially censors who printed items that reflected their own viewpoints," while the press continually "played the dual role of shaping and reflecting public opinion."[11] Yet, newspapers must rely on sales; if they are in business over a long period of time, it is safe to assume that they are either providing the perspective the purchasers want to read or are subtly shaping the reader's perspective to the philosophy of the newspaper. In any event, historians can, and should, rely on newspapers as a glimpse into the popular opinions of the day, taking into account the partisan nature of the press at that time.

With respect to local newspapers during this period, four were published in Frederick City: the *Examiner*, the *Herald*, the *Maryland Union*, and the *Republican Citizen* (frequently referred to as the *Citizen*). In the county, the *Valley Register* was published in Middletown and the *Family Visiter* in Mechanicstown (Thurmont). Most researchers have relied very heavily on the *Examiner*, largely because it is the most accessible, available at the local library. The *Republican Citizen* is as well, but only one issue is available for this time period. Most of the remainder of the newspapers are no longer available, but a few copies of the *Herald* can be found at the Maryland State Archives.

Despite the dearth of source material, enough information exists to draw several conclusions about the presidential election of 1860 in Frederick County. As Chart 1 indicates, candidate Abraham Lincoln managed only 103 votes in all of Frederick County. Ironically, the voting districts in which he received the highest total number of votes were Emmitsburg (17) and Jackson (16), both of which voted overwhelmingly for Breckenridge.

Mid-Maryland: A Crossroads of History

The 1860 Presidential Election Results in Frederick County by Voting Districts[12]

	Bell	Breckinridge	Douglas	Lincoln
Buckystown	170	109	14	3
Catoctin	58	130	17	7
Creagerstown	199	110	18	1
Emmitsburg	152	323	18	17
Frederick, East Polls	284	251	37	5
Frederick, West Polls	551	553	92	11
Hauvers	46	154	27	3
Jackson	84	195	6	16
Jefferson	140	93	16	1
Johnsville	197	71	0	3
Liberty	295	146	24	2
Mechanicstown	182	189	7	6
Middletown	330	148	27	11
Mt. Pleasant	162	76	4	0
New Market	270	179	39	10
Petersville	169	103	48	0
Urbana	144	155	7	0
Woodsboro	191	185	38	5
TOTALS:	3,617	3,170	439	103

Lincoln was viewed with distrust by both the *Examiner* and the *Herald*. As noted by the *Herald*:

> it will be seen that the Baltimore Patriot has been officially denounced [by the Constitutional Union Party's executive committee in Baltimore] as an enemy sailing under false colors. This is right, and we sincerely hope that the committee will keep on, in this good work, until the Union Party of Maryland is entirely purged of every stain of Black Republicanism from which, in past years, it has suffered no little. We never doubted that it was sound to the core on the rights and institutions of the South, while true as steel to the Union.[13]

One of the primary reasons that the Republicans were distrusted was because of their perceived sectional stance and their unwillingness to protect Southern interests. As the *Examiner* noted, "A survey of political parties discloses the fact that there is but one national party in existence [e.g., the Constitutional Union Party]. Republicanism is avowedly sectional; its principles, its policy, its purposes have a limited scope, not common to the people of all the States. The success of such a party is so repugnant to the theory of our gov't that every conservative citizen would find cause to deplore it."[14] And the *Examiner* was not alone. In a series of articles describing the founding of the Union and expounding on its virtues, the *Herald* declared that the Republicans were "the worst party that this country ever [had]."[15] And after the election on November 6, "Mr. Lincoln has been elected by a strictly sectional party, upon a strictly sectional platform, for the purpose of inaugurating a strictly sectional policy in the general government. Not a single electoral vote will he get in a slaveholding state."[16] In fact, the animosity was so intense against Lincoln that the editor of the *Herald* commented that he observed a notice in the Middletown *Valley Register* calling for a number of meetings of the Republicans in Frederick and Washington Counties. He assumed it was "a hoax….The Black Republican traitors in Maryland are bold and impudent enough in all conscience, but not quite impudent enough to hold meetings in the conservative counties of Washington and Frederick. Traitors are for the most part cowards, and they are not quite prepared for the indignation of the chivalrous people of Maryland."[17]

Stephen Douglas, the Northern Democrat, fared better than Lincoln in Frederick County, but still lacked even minimal support. He received only 439 votes in the county. Frederick City provided the strongest base of support for Douglas, but it was still under 10 percent of the city vote. He received scant votes in the election districts of Urbana (7), Mt. Pleasant (4), Mechanicstown (7) and Jackson (6). In the Johnsville election district, even Lincoln defeated Douglas, 3 votes to none.

Douglas was the first presidential candidate to "stump" across the country, giving speeches, shaking hands and meeting the people. During the campaign, the Northern Democrats portrayed their candidate as "a champion of reason between the radicals of both sections. [Douglas] was to make war boldly against *Northern abolitionists* and the Southern Disunionists, and give no quarter to either."[18] But his attempt to portray himself as a middle-of-the-road candidate failed miserably in Frederick County.

Douglas came to Frederick on September 5, 1860, and stayed at the City Hotel on West Patrick Street, where he greeted a number of citizens. In the afternoon, the candidate addressed an audience at the Court House Square and was followed by other speakers supporting his candidacy for president.

Mid-Maryland: A Crossroads of History

While Engelbrecht did not provide exact figures in his journal, he noted that "there was a large assembly present."[19] The newspaper accounts of Douglas's visit and his campaign in general did not contain the rancor present in accounts of Lincoln and the Republicans. For the most part, Douglas was virtually ignored by the Frederick press. The only references to Douglas were in the *Examiner*, which accused the Democratic presidential candidates of having "no higher ambition than mutual destruction." According to this account, both Douglas and Breckinridge "stand before the bar of public opinion, accused of conspiracy against the Union!" The *Examiner* accused Douglas of being "an advocate of Squatter Sovereignty, which is Republicanism in disguise."[20] In reading the newspaper accounts, it is apparent that Douglas was not perceived to be as threatening as was Lincoln, but it was feared that Douglas, through his own hubris, could destroy the Union.

Again examining Chart 1, it is clear that Bell and Breckinridge dominated the votes in Frederick County. While Lincoln and Douglas garnered approximately 15 percent of the votes, Bell and Breckinridge fairly split the remaining 85 percent, with Bell taking a slight majority. As one historian noted, "The contest soon resolved itself into a two-party campaign in each section: Lincoln versus Douglas in the North and Breckinridge versus Bell in the South."[21] Frederick County certainly fit this pattern.

Both the *Examiner* and the *Herald* supported the candidacy of the Constitutional Union's John Bell. The *Examiner* carried articles from the North and the South in support of Bell. The *Herald* was more strident in its defense of Southern rights, printing numerous letters from Southerners and Southern nationalists.[22] Yet it is clear that both publications supported Southern rights and believed that Bell was the candidate best able to defend those rights within the framework of the Union.

Repeatedly, Bell was presented as the national candidate, as opposed to all of the others, who were seen as sectional candidates. Again, the *Herald* commented that it "…is plain to see that the Black Republican party is the true disunion party of the country—the only party whose success would place the country in a position which would give any state in the Union a reason or plausible excuse for an attempt at secession."[23] Breckinridge, too, lacked national support according to the *Examiner*: "How is the South to maintain her Rights and avert the threatened aggression? Can she do it by voting for Breckinridge?" No, argued the editor; even if all Southerners voted for him, Breckinridge still would not have the votes to win the election and secession would result.[24] And, as noted earlier, Douglas was seen as an inadequate candidate due to his defense of popular sovereignty.

Which was the party that could defuse the crisis facing the country? The *Herald*'s answer: the Union Party, "now the only national party in the country—true the standard committed to those noble patriots—the Union nominees [Bell and Edward Evertt from Massachusetts], is the only one now waving in the breeze, that has the slightest chance of being borne aloft in triumph over the hosts of Black Republicanism."[25]

Both the *Herald* and *Examiner* urged voters to remember the election of 1856, when the Democratic candidate James Buchanan had been engaged in struggle with the newly-emergent Republican Party's candidate, John C. Fremont. The Democrats had been able to win the election, according to the two Frederick papers, only because some voters, concerned that Buchanan and third-party candidate Millard Fillmore would split the vote and thus allow Fremont to win the election, shifted to the Democratic ledger. The Democrats should now return the favor and vote for Bell, thus preventing another Republican candidate from achieving the presidency.[26]

But why support Bell and Evertt on their own merits? As the *Herald* announced on the eve of the election:

> *VOTE FOR BELL & EVERTT, and you will please your wife*
> *VOTE FOR BELL & EVERTT, and your lady love will smile upon you*
> *VOTE FOR BELL & EVERTT, and you will be proud of that vote*
> *VOTE FOR BELL & EVERTT, if you want a guarantee that the South*
>   *And its institutions will be protected*
> *VOTE FOR BELL & EVERTT, if you are opposed to DISUNION or*
>   *SECESSION*[27]

Bell and Evertt, according to the two papers, would defend Southern rights. The *Examiner*, in analyzing the upcoming election, illustrated how Bell and Evertt could win the election (as noted above) and posed the question: if the Constitutional Union Party wins, how could the South lose? Touted the *Herald*:

> *Let the Northern Union men be persuaded that Bell & Evertt have Southern strength sufficient with what Northern aid they can give them, and they will strike such a blow as will shatter Republicanism to atoms. They are waking up to a true sense of their duty & their danger; and with some encouragement from their Southern Brethren, they will come in overwhelming force to the rescue of the Union Constitution from the destructive grasp of treachery & fanaticism.*[28]

Mid-Maryland: A Crossroads of History

And Breckinridge Democrats could feel secure in their voting for Bell, "without a sacrifice of their peculiar doctrines upon the slavery question, and without the slightest shadow of distrust in regard to their fealty to the constitutional rights of the South—Mr. Bell is himself a slaveholder —an advocate of the institution in the broadest sense, and a true southern statesman." While there was less enthusiasm for Evertt from Massachusetts, "whatever his private views

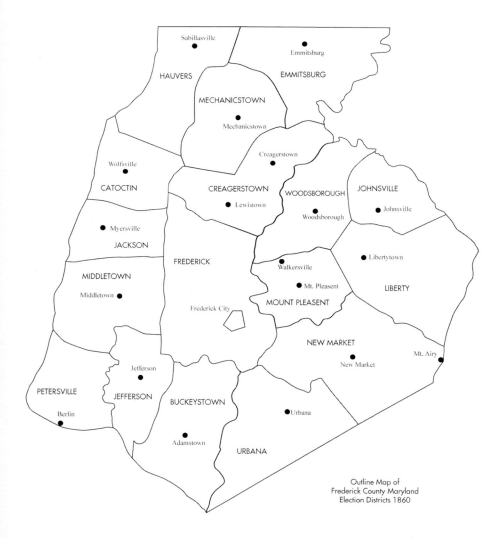

Map of voting districts in Frederick County, 1860. *Courtesy of the Historical Society of Frederick County.*

upon the abstract question of slavery," he had never violated the slogan of the party: The Union, the Constitution and the Enforcement of the Laws.[29]

A number of parades and rallies were held in Frederick for the Constitutional Union candidates. On September 6, 1860, a Bell and Evertt parade, consisting of over a hundred vehicles and three bands, was over one mile long. According to Jacob Engelbrecht, the entire procession took over sixteen and a half minutes to pass. On November 5, another parade was held in support of the Constitutional Union Party, with speeches again at the Court House Square.[30]

The Breckinridge supporters also held several processions in Frederick in support of their candidate. On September 29, William Yancey, a fire-eater from Alabama, addressed a crowd at the Court House Square. Subsequent processions were held on November 1 and November 5.[31] Unlike the Douglas rally, the Breckinridge rallies, along with those for Bell, reflected the energy and support of their constituencies in Frederick County.

An examination of the distribution of votes shows (see top page 78) that Bell captured more districts (11) than Breckinridge (7). And in taking the election districts of Frederick and Urbana, Breckinridge won areas with a high percentage of slaves. These results were to be expected.

However, a closer examination reveals some extraordinary findings. How does one explain Breckinridge's victories in Emmitsburg, Hauvers, Jackson, Catoctin and Mechanicstown (his only narrow victory of these five districts)? These are mountainous districts with little slavery. In fact, as illustrated by the bottom illustration on page 78, Hauvers and Jackson had no slaves identified in the 1860 census. There were no plantations in these districts. They lacked the wealth or property for their residents to be considered among the planter elite. These voting patterns are absolutely contrary to expectations. In addition, the mountainous regions of Virginia, North Carolina, Tennessee, Georgia and Alabama tended to vote for Bell, or even Douglas in some areas. Yet in these districts in Frederick County, Breckinridge, the candidate identified closest with the defense of Southern interests, including slavery, beat the field overwhelmingly. The reason for this ambiguity is unclear, but voting in Frederick County clearly ran counter to the trend of most other Southern voting districts.

What is clear, however, is that those in Frederick County who voted were strongly supportive of the South and her institutions, and voted for the candidate whom they believed would best defend those interests. Most voters selected a candidate whose party did not take an assertive position on slavery and its extension into the territories, but who was presented as a defender of the

Mid-Maryland: A Crossroads of History

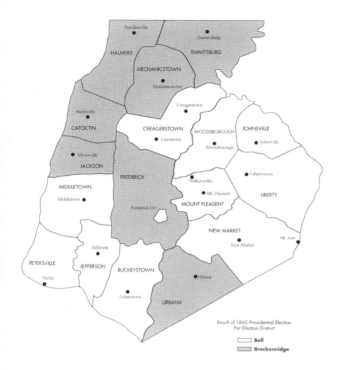

Map of the 1860 presidential election results in Frederick County by voting districts.

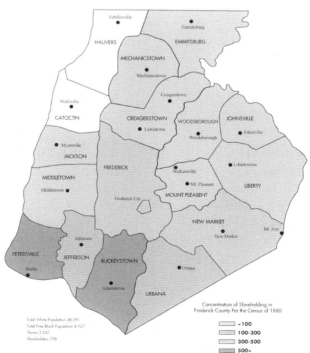

Concentration of slaves by voting districts in Frederick County according to the 1860 census.

Southern rights and interests. However, almost as many Frederick Countians voted for a candidate whose position on slavery and the extension of slavery was undeniable and whose support was ambiguous for staying in the Union if his party lost the election. Finally, as the illustrations on facing page reflect, there was little correlation between slaveholding in Frederick County and support of Breckinridge. And, contrary to other Southern states like Virginia, North Carolina, Tennessee, Georgia and Alabama, the voters in Frederick County not committed to Breckinridge were those in election districts that contained the least number of slaves. Why this is the case is not clear and may never be, due to lack of evidence.

Paul and Rita Gordon were correct in noting that "the Civil War period in Frederick County is its best kept secret."[32] Certainly the results of the election of 1860 in Frederick County can be explained to reflect a Southern county in a Southern state seeking to protect her Southern interests. The electorate decided, by a pencil-thin margin, that this protection should occur within the Union. Ripe for re-examination at this point is the depth of the Frederick County's commitment to Unionism within the context of the 1860 election results and subsequent events through the winter, spring, and summer of 1861.

Bibliography

Bestor, Arthur. "The American Civil War as a Constitutional Crisis." *American Historical Review* 69 (January 1964): 327–52.

Engelbrecht, Jacob. *Diary of Jacob Engelbrecht, 1858–1878*. Vol. 3. Frederick, MD: Frederick County Historical Society, n.d.

Fite, Emerson D. *The Presidential Campaign of 1860*. New York: The MacMillan Company, 1911.

Frederick Examiner, 1860.

Frederick Herald, 1860.

Gordon, Paul B., and Rita S. Gordon. *Never the Like Again*. Frederick, MD: Paul and Rita Gordon, 1995.

———. *A Textbook History of Frederick County.* Frederick, MD: Board of Education of Frederick County, Maryland, 1975.

Hubbell, John T. "The Douglas Democrats and the Election of 1860." *Mid-American* 55 (April 1973): 108–33.

Markell, Catherine S.T. *Diary of Catherine S.T. Markell, 1828–1900.* Frederick County Historical Society, Frederick, MD.

McPherson, James M. *Ordeal by Fire.* 3rd ed. Boston: McGraw-Hill, 2001.

Porter, David. "The Southern Press and the Presidential Election of 1860." *West Virginia History* 33 (October 1971): 1–13.

Potter, David M. *The Impending Crisis, 1848–1861.* New York: Harper & Row, 1976.

Rawley, James A. *Secession: The Disruption of the American Republic, 1844–1861.* Malabar, FL: Krieger Publishing Co., 1990.

Taylor, Lenette S. "Polemics and Partisanship: The Arkansas Press in the 1860 Election." *Arkansas Historical Quarterly* 44 (1985): 314–335.

Frederick's Confederate Son:

Bradley Tyler Johnson, Brigadier General, C.S.A.

Brian S. Baracz

I believe, if the Confederate people were true to their ideals of honor and fidelity, their glorious achievements would be certain of appreciation by the generations to come.

Bradley Tyler Johnson[1]

Bradley Tyler Johnson, born and raised in Frederick, Maryland, was a strong supporter of Southern rights. When war broke out in 1861, Johnson focused his talents on the battlefield. He proved at numerous times during the war that he was a gallant leader. Many times on the battlefield he won the praise of his superiors for his actions. When the actions of the armies led the war to Maryland, once in 1862 and again in 1864, Johnson played a pivotal role.

On September 29, 1829, Johnson was born to Charles Worthington Johnson and Eleanor Murdock Tyler. Both parents came from a very distinguished family line. Their son, Bradley Tyler Johnson, attended the Frederick Academy as well as the Rebakkah Academy in Ellicott City, Maryland, sometime between the years of 1829 and 1845. Johnson then moved on to Princeton University, where he graduated in 1849. He then studied at Harvard Law School for

Bradley Tyler Johnson. *Courtesy of the Alabama Department of Archives and History.*

two years. In 1851, Johnson was admitted to the North Carolina Bar. Jane Claudia Saunders entered Johnson's life around 1845. They were engaged for six years and, on June 25, 1851, Johnson and Saunders married. Her father held many prominent roles in the state of North Carolina and her mother was the daughter of a Supreme Court justice.[2] Jane Saunders Johnson was also a great supporter of the Confederate cause and was praised by Thomas "Stonewall" Jackson for her efforts.

Mr. and Mrs. Bradley T. Johnson had one son, Bradley Saunders Johnson, who was born around 1857.[3] Mrs. Johnson and little Bradley were often seen in the camp visiting their husband and father. "She and her escort, her little boy, were frequent visitors to the picket line, and he [young Bradley] attracted the attention and elicited the commendation of the Commanding Generals, Johnson and Beauregard, for the gallant way in which he rode with his father in front of the Yankee picket line."[4]

The years leading up to the Civil War found Johnson Sr. quite politically involved. He was the state's attorney for Frederick County. In 1859, Johnson was selected as chairman of the State Democratic Central Committee. Later in the same year he was elected as a delegate from the state of Maryland to the Democratic National Convention. The convention began in Charleston, South Carolina, and then moved to Baltimore, Maryland. With his strong support for John C. Breckinridge and the Southern Democrats, Johnson made it clear that he believed in slavery and in the states' rights philosophy. He also believed Maryland was going to side with the South during the impending war. This notion changed, however, after the election of 1860 when Augustus Bradford, a strong supporter of the Union, was elected governor of Maryland. Johnson disliked Bradford and even believed there was a plot by the governor to keep Maryland loyal to the Union. Johnson also believed that if the people of Maryland knew what was going on, they would not have any part of it and would have worked to overthrow Bradford.[5] In Johnson's mind, "Maryland thus suffered the crucifixion of the soul, for her heart was with the Confederacy and her body bound and manacled to the Union."[6]

With the winds of war swirling, Johnson started to raise a company of men from the Frederick area. The first test for these men came just hours after the firing on Fort Sumter with Abraham Lincoln's call for seventy-five thousand volunteers. The men of the North who answered the call and were ordered to defend the nation's capital made their way to Washington through parades in Boston, New York City and Philadelphia. In these cities, the troops received the ardent support of the loyal citizens. In Baltimore, however, there were no grand parades or receptions. The citizens of Baltimore greeted these Northern men with rock-throwing and gunfire. The troops traveling through Baltimore had to be transferred from President Street Station to Camden Station, the distance of about one mile, in horse-pulled cars. The people lining the streets began throwing rocks at the cars, drivers and teams. The route became so dangerous that the cars were forced to return to President Street Station. The soldiers were then ordered out of the cars and formed up to march this distance. Once again, the same angry crowd met this procession. This time, however, muskets were fired and a riot broke out on Pratt Street between troops from Massachusetts and the citizens of Baltimore. This riot continued until the police moved in and the soldiers were eventually able to reach their destination. Bradley Johnson and his minutemen received a telegram on April 19, 1861, from Marshal Kane, who was the commanding officer of the police force, stating, "Streets red with Maryland blood. Send express over the mountains of Maryland and Virginia for the riflemen to come without delay. Fresh hordes will be down on us tomorrow. We will fight them or die."[7]

On April 20, Bradley Johnson and his company arrived in Baltimore along with other companies from all around the state. Since the situation was de-escalating in Baltimore, Johnson and his men returned to Frederick without seeing any action. At the request of the states' rights members of the legislature, Johnson and his men were asked to stay in Frederick and "guard and protect them from the Unionists of the town, which were loquacious and loud in their threats against 'the Secesh.'"[8] During this stay in Frederick, Johnson trained and drilled his men into a formidable unit. Thomas J. Jackson, colonel of the Virginia Militia, was the one responsible for gathering men in this part of the state and granted permission to Johnson to move his men to Point of Rocks, Maryland. There, Johnson was to meet up with Captain Turner Ashby, who was commanding Jackson's cavalry. Johnson moved out on May 8, 1861, and by May 18 he commanded approximately 450 men. Johnson was the commander of Company A and ultimately became the regimental commander. These soldiers, proud to be from Maryland, did not recognize Virginia authorities and did not want to be placed in the Army of Virginia. Therefore, Colonel Arnold Elzey and Johnson sent their applications to Jefferson Davis to be organized separately in the Confederate army. The Marylanders wanted to fight under their own flag. Throughout the war, Johnson tried his best to make certain this was what happened.

The first test the Marylanders faced was just to survive while in camp. These "outlaws from their own state" did not have weapons, clothes, blankets, tents or cooking utensils.[9] Fortunately, Mrs. Bradley T. Johnson came to the aid of her husband and his men. On May 24, 1861, she began a three-day journey back to her home state of North Carolina to apply for arms and equipment for the men. Mrs. Johnson appeared before the governor of North Carolina, Thomas H. Ellis, and the council of the state to request equipment for these men who were willing to fight for the South. The state answered the request by giving Mrs. Johnson five hundred rifles and ten thousand cartridges with all the equipment to go with them. On the journey, she received money from the townspeople in Petersburg and Richmond. While she was in Richmond, she picked up camp supplies and ordered tents for the men. After her return to Harpers Ferry, Stonewall Jackson visited and thanked her for her work. She made another trip to Virginia for the tents she ordered. Mrs. Johnson also paid for clothes, shoes and underclothes with the money she received on the two journeys.

Bradley Johnson and the First Maryland C.S.A. would "see the elephant" at the battle of First Manassas. By the time this battle concluded, they had played a pivotal role in driving the Federals back to Washington. The First Maryland was in the Stonewall Brigade. They arrived on the battlefield at noon on July 17 and were sent to the left flank of the Confederate forces to attack the exposed flank of the Union army. The report of General P.G.T. Beauregard detailed the effect of this movement:

> [The brigade] *advanced in an irregular line, almost simultaneously, with great spirit from their several positions upon the front and flanks of the enemy in their quarter of the field. At the same time, too, Early resolutely assailed their right flank and rear. Under this combined attack the enemy was soon forced first over the narrow plateau in the southern angle made by the two roads so often mentioned into a patch of woods...The rout had now become general and complete.*[10]

After this battle, the First Maryland spent the remainder of the year near the Manassas battlefield.

Part of the military strategy of the South in the spring of 1862 was to have Stonewall Jackson make threats on Washington, hoping to draw Union forces away from their goal of moving toward Richmond. Johnson, in his *Maryland: The Confederate Military History*, wrote, "in the First Maryland, matters at this time were in very unsatisfactory condition."[11] The First Maryland was demoralized because, while enlistment for some of the men was up, all the men believed their time had been served, when it really had not. Another factor contributing to the break-down in the ranks was that the men had grown tired of army life and wanted to be back home, away from the day-to-day monotony of soldiering.

When May 23 arrived, the First Maryland was in a terrible state because of the enlistment issue. Half the men had had their rifles taken away and were being kept under guard. The regiment was moving toward its greatest moments, yet none of the men could foresee this. Two developments dramatically changed the thinking of the regiment. The first was an order from Stonewall Jackson, who wanted Johnson to take his men to the front and attack Front Royal. The second event was an address by Johnson in which he admonished his men:

> *You are the sole hope of Maryland. You carry with you her honor and her pride. Shame on you—shame on you. I shall return this order to General Jackson with the endorsement, "The First Maryland refuses to face the enemy," for I will not trust the honor of the glorious old State to discontented, dissatisfied men. I won't lead men who have no heart.*[12]

This address was remembered by George W. Booth, an officer in the First Maryland:

> *Most seething in his denunciation, and yet most feverent* [sic] *in his appeals to preserve the reputation of Maryland, his few words have been remembered by me as the most effective eloquence to which it has been my fortune to listen. Judged by the result, it transformed a body of sullen, angry and discontented men into enthusiastic, obedient soldiers, anxious to be led to the fray.*[13]

The First Maryland then advanced toward the town of Front Royal and captured the Union pickets off-guard. As these prisoners were taken back through the lines, they were questioned about their regiment. When the men heard that the Union soldiers they had captured were from the First Maryland U.S., their emotions were at a fever pitch. This advance had brought brother against brother. The First Maryland C.S.A. prevailed as men from Louisiana and Maryland forced the Federals to flee.

The next large-scale fighting the Confederates from the Old Line State saw brought praise from the Confederate high command and a trophy from the enemy. It was in this fight, near Harrisonburg, Virginia, on June 6, 1862, that the First Maryland helped carry the day, but not without loss. Out of 150 men engaged, 17 were killed or wounded and the colors went down twice, but did not hit the ground.[14] By the end of the fighting, the Maryland regiment had driven the Pennsylvania Bucktails from the field. The Marylanders retrieved discarded bucktails that the Pennsylvanians wore on their kepis. R.S. Ewell, in his official report, recognized the brave fighting done by Johnson and the regiment:

> *In commemoration of their gallant conduct, I ordered one of the captured bucktails to be appended as a trophy to their flag. The gallantry of the regiment on this occasion is worthy of acknowledgement from a higher source, more particularly as they avenged the death of the gallant Ashby, who fell at the same time.*[15]

Fighting with the Stonewall Brigade led Johnson and the First Maryland to join Robert E. Lee and take part in the Seven Days' Campaign. On June 27, 1862, the First Maryland engaged the enemy at the battle of Gaines' Mill. Once again, Johnson's leadership skills were exhibited, as evident from this account by Orderly Sergeant Robert Cushing:

> *Col. Johnson got blood up, said, "Men I have offered to lead forward the line that never yet broke—never can be broken. Forward, quick march, guide center!" The line of battle moved until with a yell we charged, and took the field sleeping on it...Our regiment has reason to be proud of its action and of its colonel.*[16]

A couple of days passed before the regiment saw action again. Even though the battle of Malvern Hill on July 1, 1862, was a defeat for the Confederates, this battle put an end to U.S. General George B. McClellan's Peninsular Campaign. During this fight, the regiment helped to repel an infantry assault that was threatening the Confederate line.

After a summer of hard campaigning, during which Johnson and the regiment won the praise of the Confederate high command time and again, this group of brave men was mustered out of service on August 16, 1862, because their enlistment had expired. This was bittersweet for both men and commander. Because of the support given to the men by Mrs. Johnson, she was presented with the First Maryland's battle flag with the bucktail still attached. After declining a possible promotion to the rank of brigadier general, Johnson was assigned to command General J.R. Jones's Second Brigade (Jones had been wounded during the Seven Days' Campaign). It was Johnson who led these men during the battle of Second Manassas, further proving his ability to command troops.

At Second Manassas, Johnson's men were positioned in the unfinished railroad cut during the fighting, where they helped to repulse Union advances.

The fighting around this railroad cut was very heavy, and Johnson wrote in his report:

> *Before the railroad cut the fight was most obstinate. I saw a Federal flag hold its position for half an hour within 10 yards of a flag of one of the regiments in the cut and go down six or eight times, and after the fight 100 dead were lying 20 yards from the cut, some of them within 2 feet of it. The men fought until their ammunition was exhausted and then threw stones.*[17]

For Johnson's actions at Second Manassas, General Stonewall Jackson once again advocated for the promotion of Johnson to brigadier general. Jackson addressed the War Department in a letter dated September 4, 1862, "So ably did he discharge his duties in the recent battles near Bull Run as to make it my duty, as well as my pleasure, to recommend him for a brigadier-generalcy."[18] Perhaps an even greater compliment paid to Johnson while commanding Jones's brigade came from Private John H. Worsham, who stated, "It was the unanimous sentiment of the Second Brigade that they were never as well handled as they were by Colonel Bradley T. Johnson, during this battle and the rest of the time he was with us."[19]

Following the victory at Second Manassas, Lee decided that the time was right to begin his first advance northward. This move by Lee culminated at Sharpsburg, Maryland, and resulted in the single bloodiest day in the history of our nation. Because the battle of Sharpsburg (better known as the battle of Antietam) occurred just over two weeks after Second Manassas, one would believe Bradley Johnson would have been in the thick of this battle on his home soil, but that was not the case. In fact, he was not even in Maryland during the battle.

When the Confederate army began its advance northward, Stonewall Jackson arranged for Bradley Johnson to meet with General Lee on the evening of September 4, 1862, at Lee's headquarters in Leesburg, Virginia. Johnson would later remember, "Gen. Lee particularly required information as to the topography of the banks of the Potomac between Loudon County, Virginia and Frederick County, Maryland, and those about Harpers Ferry and Williamsport."[20] Bradley Johnson was in command of Jones's brigade as they moved back into his hometown of Frederick on September 6, 1862, and he was made provost marshal of the town.[21]

Bradley Johnson was relieved of command of Jones's brigade on September 10, 1862, and was sent to Richmond with military dispatches. While in the Confederate capital, he was placed on the military court because of his pre-

Mid-Maryland: A Crossroads of History

Confederate soldiers marching through Frederick City on September 12, 1862. *Courtesy of the National Museum of Civil War Medicine.*

war background as a lawyer. This was Johnson's station while the Army of Northern Virginia was in his home state.

While at this position in Richmond, Johnson received the rank of colonel of cavalry on October 9, 1862. He served on this court throughout the winter of 1862 until the spring of 1863. During this time in Richmond, Johnson made good use of his position to draw support for the formation of a new regiment, called the Maryland Line. He eventually succeeded in persuading the secretary of war, James Seddon, to allow him to do this. Johnson left the court and made his way toward the army, which by this time was again moving north. On the evening of July 2, 1863, Johnson met up with the army at a small Pennsylvanian town. Due to the confusion that would have been created by Johnson taking command, he was not put in charge of troops at Gettysburg until July 4. Bradley Johnson led a brigade during the Confederate retreat after Gettysburg and crossed the Potomac with the army on July 13, 1863.[22]

The second Maryland Line was organized and included all three branches of the service, the Second Maryland Infantry, First Cavalry and the Baltimore Light Artillery. Its first orders were to move to Hanover Junction, an important rail junction for the Confederates around Richmond. While they were stationed there, General Robert E. Lee devised a plan for the Marylanders to make an attack on Point Lookout and free Confederate prisoners there. This plan never came to fruition because Union forces started to move around the junction and the Maryland Line was needed for defensive purposes.

While at Hanover Junction, Bradley Johnson learned that the Union cavalry was trying to move toward the junction and that the Federals ultimately wanted to advance on Richmond. Around March 1, 1864, Johnson moved out to halt this advance, and once again, he won the praise of his superiors. In his report, Major General Wade Hampton wrote:

> *I cannot close my report without expressing my appreciation of the conduct of Col. Bradley T. Johnson and his gallant command. With a mere handful of men he met the enemy at Beaver Dam, and he never lost sight of them until they had passed Tunstall's Station, hanging on their rear, striking them constantly, and displaying throughout the very highest qualities of a soldier. He is eminently fitted for the cavalry service, and I trust it will not be deemed an interference on my part to urge as emphatically as I can his promotion.*[23]

Major General Arnold Elzey agreed: "He and his command, the Maryland Line, have saved the city,"[24] and he issued a general order complimenting them.

Before being sent to take part in the last major Confederate push northward, Bradley Johnson finally was promoted to brigadier general. During the winter of 1863–64, Johnson had drawn up a plan to capture Abraham Lincoln while he was at the Soldiers' Home (his summer residence, where he drafted the Emancipation Proclamation). This was a very dangerous and daring plan, and Johnson had picked out two hundred of his best men for the job. After receiving approval from General Wade Hampton to begin the advance, Johnson was asked to put his plan on hold so he could aid Jubal Early in his raid on Washington.

The goal of Early's advance was to get to Washington while Bradley Johnson and his cavalry were to be sent on an impossible mission: ride approximately three hundred miles in four days, from Frederick, Maryland, to Point Lookout, Maryland, to set Confederate prisoners free. As Lee explained to President Jefferson Davis:

> *It will be well he should be a Marylander, and of those connected with the army, I consider Col. Bradley T. Johnson the most suitable. He is bold and intelligent, ardent and true, and yet I am unable to say he possesses the*

Mid-Maryland: A Crossroads of History

requisite qualities. Everything in an expedition of this kind depends upon the leader.[25]

Johnson started this ride on July 9, 1864, after securing the flank of Early in the battle of Monocacy. One of the more humorous events of the ride occurred when the Confederates passed through Owens Mill and stopped at Painter's Ice Cream store. The locals wrote, "the mountaineers thought the 'beer' was nice, but too cold, so they put it in their canteens to melt."[26]

During Johnson's ride around Baltimore in the summer of 1864, he took the war to the Maryland political leadership. The Confederates burned the home of Maryland Governor Augustus Bradford in retaliation for the burning of Virginia Governor John Letcher's home by Union General David Hunter. Bradley Johnson and his party got to within eighty miles of Point Lookout when they were called back. Even though Early prevailed at Monocacy, he was held up long enough to allow Union reinforcements to begin their move toward reinforcing the capital.

After returning to Virginia with Jubal Early, Johnson and his men were sent, under the command of General John McCausland, to the small Pennsylvania town of Chambersburg. The Confederates reached Chambersburg on July 30, 1864, and demanded $100,000 in gold or $500,000 in greenbacks. After approximately two hours of waiting, this small town was unable to come up with the ransom money, and, as a concerned Bradley Johnson wrote, "in 5 minutes the town was ablaze at over 20 different parts."[27] The actions taken at Chambersburg were just the beginning of a stormy relationship that transpired between Johnson and McCausland. The differences in how each believed a command should be handled led to the deterioration of this relationship.

The Johnson-McCausland relationship was further strained at Hancock, Maryland. McCausland, once again, made an outrageous demand on the town that included the sum of $30,000 and cooked rations for five thousand men. The town would be torched if this demand was not met. Hancock had many Southern sympathizers and Johnson argued with McCausland over this unreasonable demand placed on a town with a population of only seven hundred. The heated argument between the two was broken up only by the appearance of Union troops, which forced a Rebel withdrawal, and Hancock was spared.[28]

The late summer of 1864 produced one of the lowest points for Johnson during his Confederate service. At Moorefield, Virginia on August 7, Union cavalry surprised Johnson's brigade and "many of the First and Second Maryland awoke and gave up without firing a shot."[29] The Union forces took hundreds of prisoners, mostly Marylanders, and gathered four hundred horses. Johnson contested that the troops were camped and posted as instructed by General McCausland, but there was no help sent by the general, who was asleep three miles away at the time of the attack. As a result, Johnson bore the burden of the blame for this loss from the Confederate high command.

Johnson tried to clear his name by asking for an inquiry, but this request fell on deaf ears. Johnson then used his official report to not only give details of the actions committed by McCausland and his men, but also to once again ask for a court inquiry of investigation.

> *It is due to myself and the cause I serve to remark on the outrageous conduct of the troops on this… Every crime in the catalogue of infamy has been committed, I believe, except murder and rape. Highway robbery of watches and pocket-books was of ordinary occurrence; the taking of breast-pins, finger-rings, and earrings frequently happened…I believe a higher tone of morals and discipline may be infused in any Confederate soldier which will restrain him from disgracing himself and his countrymen by such deeds. Had there been less plunder there would have been more fighting at Moorefield on Sunday, August 7th. I tried, and was seconded by almost every officer of my command, but in vain, to preserve the discipline of this brigade…In view of the necessity that the public service demands of the investigation of this whole matter, and that the responsibility for the Moorefield disaster be placed where it belongs, I respectfully ask that a court of inquiry be convened at once.*[30]

The losses suffered by the Maryland Line at Moorefield extinguished any hopes of continuing the organization of the famed group. Because of consolidation in the army and because he was the junior officer, there was no command left for Johnson in the late summer of 1864. He was then sent to North Carolina to take over at the prison in Salisbury. His reputation was that he treated the Union soldiers there as best as circumstances would allow.

The war officially came to an end for Bradley T. Johnson on May 1, 1865, when he surrendered the prison. Following the war, Johnson stayed in Richmond and renewed his law practice. He also continued to be a strong supporter of the Confederate Lost Cause. Johnson prepared numerous articles and spoke at many reunions in the years that followed the war. Once again, he became involved in politics and was elected a senator from Virginia. Johnson moved back to his home state of Maryland in 1878, where he spent the rest of his days. Bradley T. Johnson passed away in 1903. He was laid to rest in Loudon

Mid-Maryland: A Crossroads of History

Park Cemetery in Baltimore, Maryland, on October 7, 1903. Many of the men who had served under him were present to bid him a final goodbye.

Numerous times throughout his career Bradley T. Johnson displayed the leadership qualities that won him praise from some of the most prestigious generals in the history of the Confederacy. Throughout the war, Johnson kept the spirit of the Confederate States alive in Maryland by leading Marylanders on battlefield after battlefield. In one of his many addresses after the war, Bradley Johnson said, "The causes of the Civil War are sinking out of memory, the passions aroused by it on both sides have died out, but the record of the valor, the patriotism and the endurance developed by it, will be perpetuated for generations."[31] Today, we should not let the debate over the causes of the war interfere with our recognition of these great heroes, both of the North and of the South.

Bibliography

Alexander, Charles T. "McCausland's Raid and the Burning of Chambersburg." PhD diss., University of Maryland, 1988.

Booth, George Wilson. Papers. Maryland Historical Society. Baltimore, MD.

———. *Personal Reminiscences of Maryland Soldier in the War Between the States*. Baltimore: Fleet, McGinley and Company, 1898.

Davis, Lydia. "Bradley T. Johnson, Brigadier-General, C.S.A." PhD diss., Virginia Tech University, 1973.

Early, Jubal. Jubal Early's Raid Folder. Antietam National Battlefield. Sharpsburg, MD.

———. Jubal Early's Raid Folder. Monocacy National Battlefield. Frederick, MD.

Freeman, Douglas Southall. *Lee's Lieutenants*. New York: Charles Scribner's Sons, 1943.

Goldsborough, W.W. *The Maryland Line in the Confederate Army: 1861–1863*. Baltimore: Guggenheimer, Weil and Co., 1900.

Civil War Era

Harsh, Joseph. *Taken at the Flood: Robert E. Lee and the Confederate Strategy in the Maryland Campaign of 1862*. Kent, OH: Kent State University Press, 1999.

Hennessy, John J. *Return to Bull Run: The Campaign and Battle of Second Bull Run*. New York: Simon and Schuster, 1993.

Johnson, Bradley T. *An Address Delivered at the Dedication of the Confederate Monument at Fredericksburg, Virginia*. Baltimore: Wilson H. Mules and Company, 1891.

———. "Address on the First Maryland Campaign." *Southern Historical Society Papers* 12 (1876–1953): 500–535.

———. *Maryland: The Confederate Military History*. Atlanta: Confederate Publishing Company, 1899.

———. "A Memoir of Jane C. Johnson." *Southern Historical Society Papers* 19 (1876–1953): 73.

———. Papers. Antietam National Battlefield. Sharpsburg, MD.

———. Papers. Frederick County Historical Society. Frederick, MD.

———. Papers. Maryland Historical Society. Baltimore, MD.

———. Papers. Monocacy National Battlefield. Frederick, MD.

Krick, Robert K. *Conquering the Valley: Stonewall at Port Republic*. New York: William Morrow and Company, Inc., 1996.

Ruffner, Kevin Conley. *Maryland's Blue and Gray: A Border State's Union and Confederate Jr. Officer Corps*. Baton Rouge: Louisiana State University Press, 1997.

Tanner, Robert G. *Stonewall in the Valley: Thomas J. Stonewall Jackson's Shenandoah Valley Campaign, Spring 1862*. Mechanicsburg, MD: Stackpole Books, 1996.

U.S. War Department. *The War of the Rebellion: A Compilation of the Official Records of the Union and Confederate Armies*. 128 vols. Washington, D.C.: U.S. Government Printing Office, 1880–1901.

War on the Homefront:

Sharpsburg Residents during the Battle of Antietam

Edith Wallace

Washington County is often referred to as the "Crossroads of the Civil War." The National Road and the Winchester Pike (Route 11), which cross the county east to west and north to south, respectively, were the oft-traveled routes of both the Union and Confederate armies. Also, Washington County was a border county in a border state, adjoining Pennsylvania on the north and Virginia on the south. The people of the county were therefore at the crossroads of political thought as well, almost equally divided between those in support of Lincoln's Union and those espousing at least sympathy with the South if not outright support of the Confederacy. On September 17, 1862, the nation, including Washington County, crossed a threshold into a changed and increasingly brutal Civil War.

No individuals faced the reality of the effects of war on civilians more intimately than the residents of the Sharpsburg area in September 1862. Their homes and farms were damaged and their lives forever changed not only by the ferocious battle, but also by the events that took place both before and afterward. The task of studying the battle of Antietam is not simply to understand the

Sharpsburg in 1863. *Courtesy of the Maryland Historical Society.*

Mid-Maryland: A Crossroads of History

actions of generals and the movement of troops. Understanding the impact of civil war on the civilians who were inevitably involved in the conflict serves as a stark reminder of the devastation of war on the homefront.

By 1860, the farms of the Sharpsburg District along the lower Antietam Creek drainage were well-established, prosperous farms, much of the land having been cultivated for more than one hundred years. While wheat was the mainstay of the region, other grains, especially corn, were beginning to show increased production. Property values were rising as well. Sharpsburg had become a busy canal and mill town, servicing the commercial needs of farmers and boatmen alike. The Potomac River Bridge, constructed at Blackford's Ferry around 1850, connected Sharpsburg, Maryland, to Shepherdstown, Virginia, enhancing commercial ties already well established between the two towns.

The population of the town of Sharpsburg in 1860 was approaching 1,000 and the district surrounding the town numbered over 2,200, including 235 free blacks. Beginning in the second quarter of the nineteenth century, slavery began to decline throughout Maryland. Slave ownership in Washington County had never been widely practiced; it was limited primarily to larger farms, mills and iron works. In 1860, however, there were at least 86 slaves living on various Sharpsburg District farms, generally 1 or 2 slaves per owner, an indication of prosperous times for the average farmer.[1]

In 1861, the busy lives of people in the Sharpsburg area began to change. The lines between Union and secessionist states were drawn between Republicans, known as "good Union men," and Democrats, who were often outright Southern sympathizers or were suspected of being secessionists. Young men from the area joined the armies of both sides. Old friends, neighbors and relatives found themselves on opposite sides of the political divide.

Jacob Miller was a prominent Sharpsburg landowner, businessman and public servant, and a vocal Democrat. He was acquainted with, and in many cases related to, many of the farmers and townspeople of Sharpsburg. Miller was also a slave owner, although the sheriff had taken most of his slaves in 1859 during an estate dispute. Miller's letters to his daughter living in Iowa through the 1850s and 1860s provide a window on domestic life in Sharpsburg during that troubled time period. His letters document the opinions and experiences of the local citizens in the year leading up to, and including, the battle of Antietam, as well as several years following the battle. On August 20, 1861, Miller described the political divisions in the Sharpsburg area resulting from what he called "this black republean warefare [sic]." He went on:

Civil War Era

> *I dreded some of our rowdies in town the*[y] *called us ceessionists and so reported us to the northeren troops and expected to see us all arrested when the northeren troops came on but they ware disapointed the offisers said they did not intend to molest any one on account of theer politicle opinon after they ware hear a while they ware better pleased with the democrats than with the Union or dis Union party as we call them and prove them to be such by being in favour of the war which is disunion it Self there can be no union between two parties when war exists between them.*[2]

Other Sharpsburg-area Democrats and Southern sympathizers included the Douglas family of Ferry Hill Plantation, which overlooked the Potomac River. Their son, Henry Kyd Douglas, served on the staff of Confederate General Thomas "Stonewall" Jackson. Jacob Grove opened his home on the Sharpsburg Square for General Robert E. Lee's council of war in September 1862.

Included among the leaders of the Republican Party in Sharpsburg was Dr. Augustin Biggs, the town physician and a slave owner himself. Dr. Biggs lived in a large, elegant stone house on the square, nearly opposite the Grove home. A half block to the east and only two doors from the home of Jacob Miller was a prominent stone house belonging to John Kretzer, a successful blacksmith and vocal Unionist.

While Sharpsburg was divided, Jacob Miller vehemently opposed the war, which he believed had been forced upon the country by the Republican Party. Miller was not necessarily a secessionist; however, preferring instead to pursue a peaceful settlement that would result in the preservation of the Union. This distinction was important in 1862, when part of General Robert E. Lee's reasoning for the invasion of Maryland was to free the border states from the Union, assuming a majority of Southern sympathizers were willing to secede and change the balance of power in the war. Lee found, however, that sympathy for the Southern cause in Maryland was apparently more cerebral than secessionist.

In September 1862, word had reached the people of the Sharpsburg District of the Confederate army's arrival in Frederick and its march west to South Mountain. They heard the cannons pounding the mountain to the east of Boonsboro and prepared for the coming battle. The season's wheat crop had been harvested, but the corn was still ripening in the fields. Nothing could be done to protect the crops in the fields from the impending battle. The family farms of Poffenberger, Nicodemus, Miller, Roulette, Mumma, Piper, Sherrick and Otto would soon host the two opposing armies.

Mid-Maryland: A Crossroads of History

The citizens sought cover from the fray in a variety of places. Oliver Reilly, who was six years old and living in nearby Keedysville at the time of the battle, recalled that "several hundred persons took shelter for several days at and in Killinsburg Cave, about two miles west of this town [Sharpsburg], on the day of the battle."[3] But many stayed in Sharpsburg, according to Reilly: "Mr. William Roulette, owner of the Roulette farm at Bloody Lane, during the battle September 17th was hiding in his cellar."[4] As many as two hundred people hid in the cellar of the Kretzer home.

Elizabeth Miller Blackford, Jacob Miller's daughter, chose to stay in her home in Sharpsburg. A widow, she lived with her daughters Laura, Helen, Mary and Jeannette; her young son, John Frank; and a slave named Nan. In a letter to her sister Amelia, dated February 8, 1863, Elizabeth described in detail her experience during the battle:

> *I had determined to remain at home and go in the Seller, there was two of the Dr's Darby & Tailor, from Louisiana bourded with us during their stay, they came in when about to move their wounded and prevailed on us to leave I was standing at the window when a shell exploded in Mr Russel's house between the roof and ceiling sent the shingles fliying every direction cut several rafters in two and splintered others some pieces made holes in the chimeny and out at the gable end, one piece went in the flore driveing the end of a feather bolster in so tight they could scarcely get it out, it was that, that unnerved me at the moment. I gave way and we left going out the back way to Gerry Groves Town woods, with the shells fliying over our heads and around us, we were in more danger than if we had staid at home…we went to Stephen Groves in an Ambulance from the woods passing through several Regiments, poor men marching in to battle.*[5]

Various Sharpsburg residents recounted similar stories—an image difficult to fathom when one walks the quiet streets of Sharpsburg today.

Following the battle of September 17, 1862, residents and soldiers faced a field covered with bodies, both dead and injured. As quickly as possible, wounded soldiers were removed to the makeshift hospitals set up in nearly every available building and yard. According to Captain Louis Duncan of the medical department, during the war all farmhouses north and northeast of Sharpsburg were used as hospitals.[6] Barns, granaries, sheds and tents were also used to house the wounded. Many references to hospitals appear in claims submitted by citizens to the Federal government for compensation:

> *John C. Middlekauff, claim #320, "Use of House yard barn furniture beds etc. for Hospital from Sept 16th to Oct 6th."*
>
> *Joseph Stonebraker claim #173, "Boarding and use of rooms for hospital for seventeen sick men 2 days."*
>
> *Peter Beeler, claim G-1771, "use of House 6 weeks as a Hospital."*
>
> *John Otto, claim G-1857, "My House Barn & Granary were taken possession of Sept 17th and used for Hospital purposes til the 4th of Nov. 1862."*
>
> *Philip Pry, claim G-2697, ". . . seeks compensation for 15,000 feet of prime pine plank . . . alleged to have been taken on or about 20th to 30th of September 1863[1862] by Medical Director Dr. Rauch for building Hospitals."*[7]

After the injured were removed from the battlefield, the dead had to be contended with next. The enormous number of bodies, estimated at around five thousand, must have been intimidating. Quick burial was necessary to avoid the spread of deadly diseases such as typhoid fever and cholera.[8] For this reason, the fallen soldiers were buried essentially where they lay, making the farm fields of Sharpsburg a temporary cemetery. William Roulette's damage claim, filed November 1, 1862, included "Buriel [sic] ground for seven hundred Soldiers." Samuel Mumma claimed $150.00 for "Land damaged by traveling & Buriel [sic]."[9] Such fields were difficult to cultivate until the bodies were removed and placed in permanent cemeteries beginning in 1866. John Trowbridge, a visitor to Washington County in 1865, recalled a conversation with a Sharpsburg farmer:

> *"A power of them in this here field!...I always skip a Union grave when I know it, but sometimes I don't see 'em, and I plow 'em up."...Torn rags strewed the ground. The old ploughman picked up a fragment. "This here was a Union soldier. You may know by the blue cloth."....We found many more bones of Union soldiers rooted up and exposed.*[10]

Disease did become a serious problem for the people living in the area of the battlefield in the months following the battle. Daniel Miller, whose farm was located on the northern edge of the battlefield, was Jacob Miller's older brother. In a letter dated December 7, 1862, Jacob wrote about the death of his brother, personalizing battle-related disease:

> *Your Unkle Daniel Miller is no more. He departed from us on Sunday 16th day of November last…He was not well when he left home, the day before the big battle which came off the 17th of September. When he came back he went to Henry Newkirks and continued there the balance of his time…after he got back he was taken with a diarear which was a very common complaint with the troops and Citizens…*[Daniel] *was 84 years of age the 12th day of September last.*

Miller then continued with news of other local families suffering similar losses:

> *Mrs. Adam Michael is no more she took her flite this day a weak her oldest daughter had just gon before her about eight or ten days, the other daughter and Kalille wore both down and verry ill at the same time but are geting better,—Hellen and Janet have had a severe attack of tayfoy fevour but are both geting better…Jacob* [Mumma] *and Annmarys children nearly all or perhaps all had Scarlet fevour but are all geting well—Henry Mummas wife is no more, she departed this life about two weaks since she had the same fevour….Many other citizens and hundreds of soldiers have been taken with the same, and many died, it is an army disease thus ads an addition to the Horrers of war.*[11]

The illness and death experienced by the local citizens of Sharpsburg were not circumstances for which the Federal government could provide compensation. In addition, residents found later that they would receive no restitution for much of the material damage they suffered.

The U.S. Army Quartermaster Claims reveal the enormous property losses the people of the Sharpsburg area suffered—a result of both the battle and the month-long encampment of the Federal troops. Shortly after the battle of Antietam, Major General Fitz John Porter, who was in command of the Fifth Army Corps at Sharpsburg issued Special Order No. 136. This order created "A Board of survey…for the purpose of appraising and ascertaining, if possible, the amount of damages accruing to certain property in this vicinity by troops in the service of the United States."[12] The Antietam Board of Survey personally visited the farms and homes of the citizens of Sharpsburg beginning on October 1, 1862, just two weeks after the battle. The board recorded hospital claims, physical damage to buildings and furnishings, as well as claims for crops and

CIVIL WAR ERA

Reel barn damaged during the battle of Antietam. *Courtesy of the Antietam National Battlefield, National Park Service.*

animals appropriated by Federal troops, known as quartermaster stores. On October 23, 1862, the Antietam Board of Survey reports were forwarded to Brigadier General Rufus Ingalls, chief quartermaster of the Army of the Potomac. Ingalls's reply to these reports was an indication of the difficulties the people of Sharpsburg would face in their attempts to receive compensation for the terrible damages inflicted on their property during the battle:

> *I am well aware that the loyal people of this section of Maryland have suffered severely during this campaign and doubtless to any extent beyond any relief they will ever obtain. I regret that they cannot receive full compensation now for their losses, but no disbursing officer with this Army is authorized to pay any claims for damages.* [Ingalls's emphasis][13]

Very few of the 1862 claims were settled quickly. Alfred Poffenberger, a tenant farmer on the Mary (Grove) Locher farm, received his "Treasury

Mid-Maryland: A Crossroads of History

Settlements" in 1867 and 1869 for claims that included wheat, hay, corn and rye taken between September 20 and 27, 1862, and on September 30, 1862. Although Poffenberger's house and barn were on the western edge of the West Woods, the site of some of the fiercest fighting during the morning phase of the battle, no claims for structural property damage were included in either claim.[14] One of the more poignant of these early claims was from Jacob Myers, a tenant farmer living in the area of the Mumma and Roulette farms. Myers's claim was for "Hogs, Bacon, Poultry Toole [sic] & Household & Kitchen furniture Clothing &c $82.47." The members of the Board of Survey noted, "we was at the house of Mr. Myers and seen his bill and found he had lost all he had of property…we awarded to Jacob Myers $82.47."[15]

Most of the early claims were resubmitted in the 1870s, minus the structural property damage, and included claims for hay, corn, wheat, fodder, oats, rye, fence rails, cordwood and animals. Claimants were required to prove their loyalty to the Union, a difficult task in Maryland, where all were suspect. They were also asked to produce receipts or vouchers for the stores taken. These receipts or vouchers were actually rarely given, as explained by John Otto in his 1873 claim: "The property was taken during the progress of and soon after the battle of 'Antietam,' then and there being fought, it was impossible to obtain vouchers for stores taken, or to find out the names of the officers under whose direction they were taken."[16]

The claim process was so difficult in fact, many claims were not settled until the 1880s. Some claims, including those of Jacob Miller, his sons Morgan and Andrew Rench Miller, Samuel Mumma and Henry Piper, went to the Congressional Court of Claims in 1888. This was the last resort for restitution for property damage or disallowed claims. Mumma's and Piper's claims included substantial property damage, and the Miller family likely had difficulty proving their loyalty. A note on the Morgan and Andrew Rench Miller record read "1889 still no action taken."[17]

The Quartermaster Claims submitted by the citizens of the Sharpsburg District ranged in amounts from $7,472 for Samuel Mumma, whose farm was destroyed, to the meager $82.47 claimed by Jacob Myers. Most claimants, when and if they finally received their reimbursements, were given about half the amount claimed. Much of what was claimed was taken in the months of Federal encampment around Sharpsburg following the September battle, as described by Jacob Miller in an October 1862 letter:

> *The Federal troops are encamped from Harpers Ferry to Hancock, some places thicker than others. Around town they are very thick, the outlots are full.*

The Groves & farms are all full our wilson farm is full Ottos and Shericks farms are full…they have taken all the hay within their reach they have taken about 30 tons from us about the same quanty from Francis and 80 tons from Morgan and [Andrew] rench they have taken every corn field within their reach fodder and all. Have taken all our potatoes not only ours but every bodys within their range. So I suppose we will have to send out to you for potatoes and corn this winter.[18]

Miller's last statement sheds light on an important aspect of the impact this battle had on the citizens of Sharpsburg and the surrounding area. Much of what was taken by the army in September, October and November 1862 was not just of commercial value to the farmers but included their subsistence stores for the coming winter, especially the cordwood, potatoes, apples, feed grain and animal stock. For example, John Otto claimed that "the thirteen cords of wood charged for was cut and seasoned and was piled up in my yard for winter use at the farm near Burnside Bridge."[19] The people of Sharpsburg faced a difficult winter with less than a month to prepare. The long Federal encampment also prevented many of the farmers from planting their commercial wheat crop. Jacob Miller noted in a December 1862 letter, "we have nine acres wheat down on all of our land and if the army had not been hear I would have had upward of a hundred. Many of the farmers have not sown a handfull."[20]

Finally, the citizens of Sharpsburg were affected not only by the physical damage of the battle of Antietam, but also by the political ramifications that emerged as a result of the battle. In the North, political opposition to Lincoln and the Republican Party's handling of the war had been growing. The Copperhead or "peace Democrat" movement of the Democratic Party, espoused in Jacob Miller's letters, and expressed in McClellan's defensive approach to battle, had increasingly become a problem for Lincoln and his staff. Following the "victory" of the Union forces at Antietam, President Lincoln felt the time was right to issue the Emancipation Proclamation. By freeing the slaves in the secessionist states, Lincoln effectively ended any chance for the peaceable compromise so hoped for by the Copperheads of the North and the less-hawkish members of the Confederacy, and set the stage for the brutal warfare waged by Grant and Sherman.[21]

On September 24, 1862, shortly following the issuance of the preliminary Emancipation Proclamation, in a move that further changed the face of the North-South conflict for civilians, Lincoln suspended the writ of habeas corpus.[22] This consolidated power in the Federal government and put in jeopardy those citizens who might have opinions different from those of their Republican neighbors. The effect in Sharpsburg was felt almost immediately in October of 1862, when the Reverend Robert Douglas, father of Confederate officer Henry Kyd Douglas, was arrested on suspicion of signaling the enemy across the Potomac River from a window in his home at Ferry Hill. After some allegedly rough treatment in Brunswick and at Fort McHenry over a six-week imprisonment, the provost marshal released the elderly Douglas. No charges were brought against him and no evidence collected.[23]

In 1864, eighty-four-year-old Jacob Miller and four of his grown children were also harassed at the hands of the provost marshal.

> *A Squad of Soldiers came to the house and arrested Sam, Savilla & myself and took us to Harpers-ferry when we got to the mouth of the lane which leads down to the mill the lieutenant and a possy of Soldiers took that road and went on and Arrested Morgan and* [Andrew] *Rench we Stoped at antietum Bridge til they came up, then we went on to the ferry together…we ware there two & a half weaks…Captn Alexandrew who was one of Gen Hunter Staff…examined into the matter and found that there was no charge against either of us, the provost Marshal discharged us without asking a word.*[24]

Similar stories were told throughout the border states. Suspicions among neighbors concerning loyalty to the Union, however unfounded, or even revenge over a neighborly dispute could be settled through the military authority of the provost marshal.

The citizens of the Sharpsburg District suffered materially, physically and mentally as a result of the battle of Antietam. The divided nation, however, would suffer more in the years to follow as the war intensified and political differences hardened. The despair is evident in Jacob Miller's December 1862 letter:

> *That* [Republican] *party is the whole and sole cause of all our difficulties and rupture of this, of all Countries the best in the world, and I fear never will be restored, and I know never can be as it was. As to my individual interest in the settlement of this matter will amount to but little as my race is nearly run, but as to the rising generations the difference may be great.*[25]

While Jacob's opinion of the party of Lincoln was harsh, his fears of the long-term effects of the Civil War were undoubtedly echoed across the country.

Civil War Era

Bibliography

Books and articles

Barron, Lee, and Barbara Barron. *The History of Sharpsburg, Maryland.* Sharpsburg, MD: Barbara and Lee Barron, 1972.

Bell, Herbert C. *History of Leitersburg District Washington County, Maryland.* Leitersburg, MD: Published by the author, 1898; reprint, 3rd ed., Waynesboro, PA: The Caslon Press, 1985.

Burgess, John W. *The Civil War and the Constitution 1859–1865.* 2 vols. New York: Charles Scribner's Sons, 1901.

Catton, Bruce. *Mr. Lincoln's Army.* Garden City, NY: Doubleday & Co., Inc., 1951.

Clark, Linda B. *An Index to Hagerstown Newspapers.* 10 vols. 1790–1844. Hagerstown, MD: Washington County Free Library, 1982.

Douglas, William O. *Mr. Lincoln and the Negroes, The Long Road to Equality.* New York: Atheneum, 1963.

Drake, Julia Angeline, and James Ridgely Orndorff. *From Mill Wheel to Plowshare.* Cedar Rapids, IA: The Torch Press, 1938.

Frassanito, William A. *Antietam: The Photographic Legacy of America's Bloodiest Day.* New York: Charles Scribner's Sons, 1978.

Frye, Susan Winter. "Mill Settlement Patterns along the Antietam Creek Drainage, Washington County, Maryland." Master's thesis, College of William and Mary, Williamsburg, VA, 1984.

Green, Fletcher M., Thomas F. Hahn, and Nathalie W. Hahn, eds. *Ferry Hill Plantation Journal, Life on the Potomac River and Chesapeake and Ohio Canal 4 January 1838–15 January 1839.* Shepherdstown, WV: Thomas W. Hahn, 1975.

Mid-Maryland: A Crossroads of History

Hays, Helen Ashe. *The Antietam and Its Bridges, The Annals of an Historic Stream.* New York: G.P. Putnam's Sons, 1910.

Jamieson, Perry D. *Death in September, The Antietam Campaign.* Fort Worth, TX: Ryan Place Publishers, 1995.

Johnson, Robert Underwood, and Clarence Clough Buel, eds. *Battles and Leaders of the Civil War.* Vol. 2. New York: Thomas Yoseloff, Inc., 1956.

Luvaas, Jay, and Harold W. Nelson, eds. *The U.S. Army War College Guide to the Battle of Antietam, the Maryland Campaign of 1862.* Washington, D.C.: Harper Collins Publishers, 1987.

Marshall, John A. *The American Bastile: A History of the Arbitrary Arrests and Imprisonment of American Citizens in the Northern and Border States, on Account of Their Political Opinions, during the Late Civil War.* Philadelphia: Thomas Hartley & Co., 1883.

Murfin, James V. *The Gleam of Bayonets.* Baton Rouge: Louisiana State University Press, 1982.

Reilly, Oliver T. *The Battlefield of Antietam.* Sharpsburg, MD: Oliver T. Reilly, 1906.

Rice, Millard Milburn. *New Facts and Old Families from the Records of Frederick County, Maryland.* Baltimore: Genealogical Publishing Co., Inc., 1984.

Scharf, J. Thomas. *History of Western Maryland.* 2 vols. Baltimore: Regional Publishing Co., 1968.

Schildt, John W. *Four Days in October.* Chewsville, MD: 1978.

———. *Monuments at Antietam.* Frederick, MD: Great Southern Press, 1991.

Sears, Stephen W., ed. *The Civil War Papers of George B. McClellan, Selected Correspondence 1860–1865.* New York: Ticknor & Fields, 1989.

Smith, John Philemon. *Reminiscences of Sharpsburg.* 1912. Located at Washington County (MD) Free Library, Sharpsburg Branch.

Stotelmyer, Steven R. *The Bivouacs of the Dead.* Baltimore: Toomey Press, 1992.

Williams, Thomas J.C. *History of Washington County, Maryland, from the Earliest Settlements to the Present Time.* Hagerstown, 1906; reprint, Baltimore: Clearfield Co. & Family Line Publications, 1992.

Zenzen, Joan M. *Battling for Manassas.* University Park: The Pennsylvania State University Press, 1998.

Federal government files

Quartermaster Claims Files, RG 92. National Archives, Washington, D.C.

Union Provost Marshal's File, M-345, Roll 191. National Archives, Washington, D.C.

U.S. Agriculture Census, 1850–1880. Microfilm Collection, Maryland Hall of Records, Annapolis, MD.

U.S. Census of Manufactures, 1820. Microfilm, Western Maryland Room, Washington County Free Library, Hagerstown.

U.S. Manufacturing Census, 1850–1870. Microfilm Collection, Maryland Hall of Records, Annapolis, MD.

U.S. Population Census. Microfilm Collection, Washington County Free Library, Hagerstown, MD.

U.S. Slave Census, 1850–1860. Microfilm Collection, Maryland Hall of Records, Annapolis, MD.

Historic reports and surveys

"Aluminum Sided Farmhouse [Nicodemus Farm]," 1978. Maryland Historical Trust, State Historic Sites Survey Forms, Crownsville.

"Antietam National Battlefield Site," 1980. National Register of Historic Places Inventory Nomination Forms, Washington, D.C.

"Belinda Springs Farm," 1976. Maryland Historical Trust, State Historic Sites Survey Forms, Crownsville, MD.

Mid-Maryland: A Crossroads of History

"Hitt's Mill," 1977. National Register of Historic Places Inventory Nomination Forms, Washington, D.C.

Joseph, Maureen DeLay. Historic Woodlot Restoration: West Woods Antietam National Battlefield. Sharpsburg, Maryland. Eastern Team Falls Church, Denver Service Center, National Park Service, 1994.

"Log Farmhouse [Cunningham Farm]," 1978. Maryland Historical Trust, State Historic Sites Survey Forms, Crownsville, MD.

"Neikirk Farm," 1978. Maryland Historical Trust, State Historic Sites Survey Forms, Crownsville, MD.

"Otto House, 1978." Maryland Historical Trust, State Historic Sites Survey Forms, Crownsville, MD.

Reed, Paula S. "History Report: The D.R. Miller Farm Antietam Battlefield Sharpsburg, Maryland." Hagerstown MD: Preservation Associates, Inc., 1991.

———. "Keedysville Survey Report." Hagerstown, MD: Preservation Associates, Inc., 1993.

"Roulette Farm, 1978." Maryland Historical Trust, State Historic Sites Survey Forms, Crownsville, MD.

"Ruins of Log House [Locher/A. Poffenberger Farm]," 1978. Maryland Historical Trust, State Historic Sites Survey Forms, Crownsville, MD.

Wilshin, Francis F. "Historic Structures Report: Mumma 'Spring House,' Piper 'Slave Quarters,' Sherrick 'Smoke House,' History Data, Antietam National Battlefield Site Maryland." National Park Service, 1969.

Maps

Griffith, Dennis. "Map of the State of Maryland," 1794. Western Maryland Room, Washington County Free Library, Hagerstown, MD.

Lake, Griffing and Stevenson. *An Illustrated Atlas of Washington Co., Maryland*. Philadelphia: 1877. Western Maryland Room, Washington County Free Library, Hagerstown, MD.

Civil War Era

Taggert, Thomas. "A Map of Washington County," 1859. Land Records Office, Washington County Courthouse, Hagerstown, MD.

Tracey Map, early land patents of Washington County as plotted by Dr. Tracey. Western Maryland Room, Washington County Free Library, Hagerstown, MD.

Varle, Charles. "Map of Frederick and Washington Counties," Maryland, 1808. Western Maryland Room, Washington County Free Library, Hagerstown, MD.

Washington County, Maryland, government files

Chancery Court Records. Washington County Court House, Hagerstown, MD.

Land Records. Washington County Court House, Hagerstown, MD.

Land Patent Books, 1 and 2. Washington County Court House, Hagerstown, MD.

1803 Tax Assessment Record. Western Maryland Room, Washington County Free Library, Hagerstown, MD.

Tax Assessment Records, 1815, 1818, 1835, 1896. Maryland Hall of Records, Annapolis.

Wills. Washington County Court House, Hagerstown, MD.

Washington County, Maryland, sources

"Antietam Battlefield." Vertical Files, Western Maryland Room, Washington County Free Library, Hagerstown, MD.

Hagerstown Gazette, Washington County Free Library.

Letters of Jacob Miller, unbound transcribed copy, transcribed between 1993 and 1995 by Paul Chiles, Antietam National Battlefield, Western Maryland Room, Washington County Free Library, Hagerstown, MD.

Nelson, John. "Hospitals of Antietam." Lecture, Washington County Free Library, Hagerstown, MD, November 11, 1999.

"Sharpsburg." Vertical Files, Western Maryland Room, Washington County Free Library, Hagerstown, MD.

The Torchlight and Public Advertiser (Hagerstown, MD), Washington County Free Library, Hagerstown, MD.

Frederick's Citizens:

Caring for the Civil War Sick and Wounded

Kari Turner

No one could have been prepared for the horrors of the Civil War. Yet unsuspecting men and women, soldiers and citizens, North and South, were forced daily to live with the realities of war at their doorsteps. Out of these circumstances, heroes emerged. These heroes were found in towns such as Frederick, Maryland. At the time of the Civil War, Frederick City had a population of approximately eight thousand and served as the connection between Washington and Baltimore, and with Pennsylvania and points farther west and north. Many Union soldiers passed through Frederick on their way to Washington, D.C., and thousands of sick and wounded would pass through by rail. Frederick would serve as a hospital center as well. The people of Frederick, like many in Maryland, were divided in support of the armies. Whatever their sympathies, however, these were men and women whose lives were interrupted by the war and by the great number of sick and wounded that were brought to the area.

Frederick's integral involvement in the war began in 1861 with the meeting of the Maryland legislature in the city. Because of Frederick's divided loyalties,

General Hospital Number One in Frederick. *Courtesy of the National Museum of Civil War Medicine.*

Mid-Maryland: A Crossroads of History

Federal officials became anxious and suspicious of the legislature's intent. On Lincoln's orders, the Federal army arrested men deemed "enemies" of the state and prevented the legislature from voting to withdraw Maryland from the Union. Federal officials and regiments subsequently moved in and stationed themselves in the city. Frederick became an occupied town. It was a key locale for the Federal forces, especially during the Antietam Campaign,[1] not only because it was located within a border state, but also because of its close proximity to Washington, D.C. Although the town switched hands several times, Frederick was occupied by Northern forces for most of the war.

Shortly after the headquartering of the Federal forces within the city, Frederick's first Civil War hospital was established. As local historians Paul and Rita Gordon wrote, "In early August, 1861, Brigadier General Nathaniel Banks…designated Frederick as a divisional military depot and hospital."[2] The location of the hospital was selected "when Colonel George H. Crossman, Assistant Quartermaster General, arrived in Frederick on August 6, 1861, to carry out Banks' orders."[3] Colonel Crossman chose the Hessian barracks, a site near where the Potomac Home Brigade was encamped on the edge of town. The barracks were used during the Revolutionary War and stand today as part of the grounds of the Maryland School for the Deaf. This hospital became known as the U.S. General Hospital Number One and was often referred to simply as the hospital, but was also known as the General Hospital or the Barracks Hospital.

As the Antietam Campaign progressed, and the Confederate forces moved into Maryland, Frederick began to feel the effects of the war more heavily as the wounded began to pour into the city. The battle of South Mountain occurred just west of Frederick City, on September 14, 1862, followed by the battle of Antietam on September 17, 1862. These battles produced massive numbers of casualties and victims on both sides who needed the medical care Frederick's hospitals could provide. Following Antietam, Robert E. Lee and his men retreated back into Virginia under the cover of darkness, leaving their wounded and dying to be cared for by the civilians of the nearby hospitals. Because of its central location and proximity to the battles of the Antietam Campaign, Frederick became an official "hospital town." As the wounded were brought from the battlefields, the General Hospital filled as ambulances continued bringing more wounded soldiers. The Confederate presence remained in Frederick, even though most of the fighting had shifted south. Over the course of the war Frederick continued to encounter the Confederates as the city switched hands between Northern and Southern forces and the citizens strove to serve the sick and wounded of both sides. The increasing number of these soldiers necessitated the opening of additional hospitals within Frederick.

There were many ways in which the citizens of Frederick comforted the sick and wounded soldiers. Churches as well as other public buildings were converted into temporary hospitals and, in a few cases, private homes were as well. With the local regiments bringing in their sick and wounded, General Hospital Number One was soon filled to capacity (approximately seven hundred men). While the Civil War produced massive numbers of disabled soldiers, about half of those found in the hospitals were there not because of battle wounds, but due to illness. The most common of these diseases were typhoid and dysentery. However, following the major battles of the Antitam Campaign, the wounded outnumbered the ill. A letter written from Frederick following the battle of Antietam bears witness to this fact:

> *As the badly wounded who can be moved are being brought in convalescents are being sent away, and now that the railroad communication is complete, they are being sent north at the rate of about 700 a day. But no sooner are they gone than others take their place, as those that lie in Middletown and Boonsboro are brought in here, where they can be made more comfortable.*[4]

Jacob Engelbrecht, one of Frederick's civil leaders, also noted in his diary on September 18, 1862, "our City is now filled with wounded from the late Battles near Boonsborough & Sharpsburg yesterday I Counted 25 Ambulances filled with wounded to be put in the Hospital."[5] Two days later he stated that "wounded Soldiers both of ours & Rebels are arriving in our town every few hours—nearly all the Churches &c are crowded with wounded & Sick."[6] On September 30, 1862, Engelbrecht noted:

> *Our town, has been thus far perhaps the greatest Depot for the wounded. Since the Commencement of this dreadful Rebellion—we have had nearly all the wounded in the three days battles in Frederick & Washington Counties. and as the Rebels Skedaddled. after the last battle at Antietam. They left all their wounded in our hands. Since then they have been bringing to our City nearly every day—many of them as they improve & are only Slightly wounded are Sent off to Baltimore & Washington &c others again have gone home—Still we have in our City from 5 to 6000—and they are bringing from 4 to 600 every day.*[7]

Mid-Maryland: A Crossroads of History

Evangelical Lutheran Church in Frederick, facing the sanctuary, after the battle of Antietam with planks over the pews. *Courtesy of the Evangelical Lutheran Church in Frederick, Maryland.*

By late summer and early fall of 1862 there were over twenty hospitals in Frederick. These hospitals included, but were not limited to, the City Hotel (located on the corner of W. Patrick and N. Court Streets and known later as the Francis Scott Key Hotel), the All Saints Episcopal Church (located on W. Church Street across from the current City Hall), the German Reformed Church (now the United Church of Christ, located on W. Church Street between N. Court and N. Market Streets), the Trinity Chapel (located on W. Church across from the German Reformed Church), the Frederick Presbyterian Church (located on Second Street about a block behind the German Reformed Church), the Novitiate (no longer stands but was located on E. Second Street in the vicinity of St. John's Catholic Church), the Visitation Academy (still stands, and looks much the same as it did at that time, on E. Second Street), the Evangelical Lutheran Church (located on E. Church Street) and Frederick's Female Seminary (now Winchester Hall, located on E. Church Street across from the Evangelical Lutheran Church). The use of these buildings as hospitals not only prevented the citizens from using them for their intended purposes, but also caused damage that took many months to repair.

CIVIL WAR ERA

Sketch of the Frederick Presbyterian Church, used as a hospital after the battle of Antietam. Plate XXXVI in Charles F. Johnson's The Long Roll.

These additional hospitals were staffed not only with doctors and nurses, but also by civilian volunteers. Frederick had become a hospital town "filled with the wounded,"[8] and its citizens were now entrusted with the care and comfort of the soldiers who had come face to face with the grim realities of war. Many of Frederick's hospitals were temporary, open for the few months following major engagements when the need was greatest. U.S. General Hospital Number One, however, remained in operation for the entire course of the war.

The civilians received a great deal of praise in the reports and letters of the soldiers for showing compassion and making them as comfortable as possible. When the nurses did not have the extra time to listen to and talk with the soldiers, or pen a letter to families, the volunteers did. The people of Frederick rose to the occasion when they were asked to provide "chicken, eggs, butter, dried fruit, milk, corn, starch, cocoa, gelatin,...sugar, and articles of like character, such as the experience of every woman has taught her are grateful and nutritious to the sick."[9] All these staples, along with fresh vegetables, herbs and other such goods produced by the citizens of Frederick, became a major part of the soldiers' diet while in Frederick hospitals.

The women of Frederick established the Ladies Relief Association, which was founded in 1861 with the express purpose of assisting and serving the hospitals within the precincts of their city. These women, often referred to as "the good ladies of Frederick," were unflagging in their work. They sought to care and provide for the needs of the soldiers with regard to diet, raiment and emotional or spiritual strength. Like many other women throughout the county and country, Frederick's women visited the hospitals bringing food and clothing or simply offered a cheerful countenance for the sick and wounded. The Ladies Relief Association organized the work of the volunteers, ensuring that each day of the week someone would check on the soldiers' and hospitals' needs as well as distribute the goods they had gathered. As described by the Frederick *Examiner* on March 19, 1862:

> *The Relief Association of Frederick city, desires to call the attention of the loyal women to the work in which they are engaged. Since the establishment of a Hospital for sick and wounded soldiers, at this place, last August, the Association has been laboring to contribute towards the wants and comfort of its inmates. Such delicacies the sick usually obtain at home, where the hand of love and affection is ever ready to minister to the suffering, have been from day to day taken to the Hospital and have been given either to the sick or to the nurses appointed by the medical authorities of the establishment.*[10]

The October 16, 1861 edition of the Frederick *Examiner* praised the women's efforts and stated, "The ladies of Frederick are not behind their countrywomen anywhere in acts of charity or humanity, and many a convalescent soldier will bear grateful testimony to the kindness, assiduity and ample provision they have made for his comfort and restoration to health."[11]

Paying visits to the soldiers was one of the greatest comforts the women were able to provide. It was these women, one soldier stated, whose "visits to the barracks 'made the heavy walls look home-like.'"[12] In addition to the women of the city, local ministers and priests visited the soldiers in an effort to meet the spiritual needs of these men, spending time with them in prayer and providing services and sacraments. Women helped the clergy by contributing Bibles and church tracts to the hospitals.

The citizens of Frederick also volunteered to work in the hospitals. Following one of the periods of Confederate occupation of the city in which the Confederate sick and wounded were placed in the hospitals, the nurses employed by the Union army were forbidden to attend them. Caring for the Confederate soldiers by those employed in the Federal government during times of occupation by the enemy of that government would have been considered aiding and abetting of the enemy. During the brief Rebel occupation of the city, then, the task of attending the sick fell to Frederick's townspeople. As Sister Marie Louise, one of the Daughters of Charity nurses who had been hired by the U.S. government to serve at Frederick's General Hospital Number One noted in her diary: "The citizens were now at liberty to do what they pleased; they flocked in crowds to the hospital distributing food, clothing, linen, etc. at their own discretion."[13] The Novitiate students of the city readily rose to the challenge and, with assistance from the women of the town, carried on the task of caring for the sick and wounded until the Confederates withdrew, allowing the nurses to resume their duties. One man noted in a letter that, "at all hours of the day, and even at night, you can find the good ladies of Frederick at the bedside of our poor sick and wounded soldiers. The men get well rapidly under their kind treatment."[14] As Jacob Engelbrecht observed, the soldiers "are all well taken Care of by the Ladies of our town who are unremittant in their attention."[15]

Yet another example of the citizens' contributions to medical care during the war occurred at the moments when Frederick "changed hands" between the armies. Upon learning of the approach of the Confederate troops in June 1863, the Federal forces abandoned the city. Citizens assisted the government in the movement and protection of the government stores, as well as the removal of most soldiers to other hospitals in the vicinity of Washington and Baltimore. As Engelbrecht noted, "all our Government Stores, have been removed, to Baltimore, &c Nearly all the Sick & wounded have been removed from U.S. Hospital at the Barracks (Except Such, as were too Sick)—to day the Cars have Stopped running."[16]

Again on September 5, 1863, the citizens helped as the hospitals were emptied of soldiers and the Union army and hospital stores were burned to prevent the approaching Confederate forces from acquiring them. Lastly, in July 1864, the citizens demonstrated their concern for their city and its occupants as they met the ransom demands of the Confederate forces occupying the city. The Confederate army demanded a ransom of $200,000 or $50,000 worth of medical supplies in addition to other military stores, or else they would burn the town. The banks' payment of this ransom saved not only the city, the hospital and military stores, but also the soldiers in the hospital.

The citizens of Frederick continually attended to the needs of the sick and wounded soldiers. Their care of the soldiers was manifested in various ways throughout the war and always at a sacrifice to themselves. Frederick's citizens were unwavering in their devotion to the soldiers' care and comfort, and they received praise and acknowledgment for their efforts from the soldiers they served. Donating their buildings and homes for use as hospitals, visiting and nursing the soldiers, providing food and other necessities, assisting in the movement and protection of the sick and wounded during occupation by Confederate forces and raising ransom money to prevent the destruction of their town—in all these ways, the citizens of Frederick provided for the needs of the sick and wounded soldiers entrusted to their care.

Bibliography

Ashbury, John W. *And all our yesterdays: A Chronicle of Frederick County, Maryland*. Frederick, MD: Diversions Publications, Inc., 1997.

"Civil War Nurses." http://www.civilwarhome.com/civilwarnurses.html.

Markell, Catherine S.T. *Diary of Catherine S.T. Markell, 1828–1900*. Historical Society of Frederick County, Frederick, MD.

Floyd, Harriet Pettit. *Civil War Memories*. Historical Society of Frederick County, Frederick, MD.

Goldsborough, E.R. *Military Hospitals—1862*. Frederick County Points of Interest, August 4, 1936. Civil War–Hospitals Folder, Historical Society of Frederick County, Frederick, MD.

Gordon, Paul, and Rita Gordon. *A Playground of the Civil War*. Frederick, MD: M&B Printing, Inc., 1994.

———. *A Textbook History of Frederick County*. Frederick, MD: Board of Education of Frederick County, 1975.

Johnson, Charles F. *The Long Roll*. East Aurora, NY: The Roycrofters, 1911. Reprinted, Shepherdstown, WV: Carabelle Books, 1986.

Lewis, David J. *Frederick War Claim: Evidence and Argument in Support of Bill to Refund Ransom Paid by the Town of Frederick, during the Civil War, to Save Said Town and the

Civil War Era

Union Military Supplies From Destruction. Historical Society of Frederick County, Frederick, MD.

Maryland Remembers: A Guide to Historical Places and People of the Civil War in Maryland. Hagerstown, MD: Maryland Civil War Centennial Commission, 1961.

"Misinformed." *Frederick Examiner*, October 16, 1861. Civil War–Ladies Relief Society Folder, Historical Society of Frederick County, Frederick, MD.

Quynn, William R., ed. *The Diary of Jacob Engelbrecht*. Vol. 3, 1858–1878. Frederick, MD: Historical Society of Frederick County, 1976.

Sister Marie Louise. *Annals of the War: Frederick, Maryland*. Saint Joseph's Provincial House, Emmitsburg, MD. Civil War–Daughters of Charity Folder, Historical Society of Frederick County, Frederick, MD.

Steiner, Lewis H. to Col. W.P. Moulasy. September 18, 1861. Manuscript Holdings, Historical Society of Frederick County, Frederick, MD.

"To the Loyal Women of Frederick County." *Frederick Examiner*, March 19, 1862. Civil War Medicine and Sanitation Folder, Historical Society of Frederick County, Frederick, MD.

Ward, Geoffrey C., et al. *The Civil War: An Illustrated History*. New York: Alfred A. Knopf, Inc., 1990.

Williams, T.J.C. *History of Frederick County Maryland*. 2 vols. Baltimore: Regional Publishing Company, 1979.

Historic Memory and Preservation

As the pressure from development is ever increasing in Mid-Maryland, the need for architectural historians and preservationists increases as well. The most important and significant historic buildings and sites must be preserved and, if possible and desirable, restored. Local governments offer tax incentives and have created historic preservation commissions to enhance preservation in their respective jurisdictions. In Frederick County alone, the population has nearly tripled over the past forty years. During the same period, housing units more than tripled, from 21,443 in 1960 to 73,017 in 2000. Concomitantly, and not surprisingly, a decrease in both the number of farms and the acreage of farmland has occurred.[1] Although the numbers will vary, all of the counties in this region are experiencing the pressures that increased population brings. Determining what sites the community will preserve, and to what extent they are preserved, becomes increasingly challenging. Preservationists and architectural historians are essential to the identification, recordation and preservation of historically significant sites.

Katherine Grandine, a historian and senior project manager for the Frederick-based R. Christopher Goodwin & Associates, Inc., presents her investigation of one mid-nineteenth-century farm's outbuildings, and in particular analyzes the barn within the context of regional barn designs and construction. In studying various bank barn styles typical of the region, Grandine observes that the traditional bank barn was the most efficient and adapted itself well to the changing uses required of it. Although the bank barn was first introduced by the German settlers and was the dominant barn

Mid-Maryland: A Crossroads of History

style in the nineteenth and early twentieth centuries, by the 1930s, changing regulations regarding milking made this type of barn obsolete. However, these barns can still be found throughout the region today.

Paula Stoner Reed, an architectural historian, examines the *L'Hermitage*, which, according to Reed, is the "only known intact French Colonial plantation complex in Maryland." Situated on the Monocacy battlefield, *L'Hermitage* contains unique and fascinating outbuildings, and was home to the Vincendieres, who were refugee plantation owners fleeing the slave revolt in Haiti in the early 1790s. In addition to the various members of the Vincendiere family that resided at this location, other French refugees probably joined them from time to time, creating a lively connection between Frederick and the French in Haiti. This Caribbean/French/Frederick County connection is quite rare in the county. Reed notes that a descendant of the Vincendieres, Enoch Lewis Lowe, was one of the four governors of Maryland to have come from Frederick County.

Francis Zumbrun, who has been involved with the Living History Foundation of Allegany County, undertook the difficult task of locating the burial site of the early American patriot and pioneer Colonel Thomas Cresap. Through archeological evidence and with the assistance of experts, Zumbrun located Colonel Cresap's burial site and facilitated the restoration of his stone to the site, thus honoring one of Maryland's earliest heroes.

And finally, Mary McCarthy, a former resident of Frederick County and an activist on preservation issues, has prepared a how-to essay on historic preservation.[2] She covers the essentials of getting started, the most effective methods of preserving specific structures and sites, and how best to maximize publicity for one's efforts. McCarthy presents examples from across the country, but for a specific case study she examines select preservation efforts in Frederick County. McCarthy's successful efforts make her contribution especially helpful to those interested in historic preservation and how to get involved.

Cultural Resources Management:

A Delicate Balance—The Campbell Farmstead

Katherine Grandine

This paper presents the results of an in-depth investigation into the history and significance of the agricultural outbuildings associated with the Campbell Farmstead in Frederick County, Maryland. The farmstead includes a main house constructed between 1820 and 1855 as well as agricultural outbuildings ranging in date from circa 1820 through the 1930s. This investigation was part of a program of project mitigation negotiated among Riverside Investment Group LLC, the City of Frederick, and the Maryland Historical Trust pursuant to Maryland Annotated Code Article 83B. The program included stabilization and marketing of selected buildings, and recordation of the nineteenth-century barns and the wagon shed/corncrib.[1]

While preservation of the historic structure itself is generally the preferred method of historic preservation, documentation is frequently used to preserve the information value of resources that can not be retained. Documentation of the nineteenth-century Campbell Farmstead outbuildings included exhaustive historic research, measured drawings, detailed descriptions and large-format

Campbell Farm bank barn, built in 1854. *Courtesy of R. Christopher Goodwin & Associates, Inc.*

Mid-Maryland: A Crossroads of History

photography. Such studies also may explore important research questions on design, construction and modification. Recordation creates a permanent archive of the resource that is accessible to the public.

The investigation of the Campbell Farmstead agricultural outbuildings provided an opportunity to study intensively a class of buildings that are quickly disappearing from the rural landscape in Maryland. These building types frequently present limited potential for reuse due to changes in farming technology, demographics and land use. Investigation into these resources is critical to understanding their historical importance and to making informed management decisions for their future.

The Campbell property on Gas House Pike originally was part of "Addison's Choice" comprising 2,300 acres patented in 1724 by Colonel Thomas Addison. Members of the Addison family retained title to the land until 1771, when Joseph Sim bought the property.[2]

In 1794, Joseph Sim sold the property, described in the deed as his "dwelling plantation," to William Campbell of Anne Arundel County.[3] In his will dated 1821, William Campbell, age sixty-five, appointed John McHenry and his youngest son Edward (then age twenty or twenty-one) as trustees and executors to manage the estate for the benefit of Campbell's children and their heirs.[4] Campbell instructed that his debts be paid from the proceeds of the sale of properties in Baltimore County, Frederick Town and Washington, D.C. Campbell planned for his plantation, known as "The Richlands," to be divided into five parcels among his married daughter and three unmarried sons. The daughter, Catherine Cunningham, inherited Campbell's mansion house, furnishings, plate, blacksmith tools and agricultural implements.

Randolph Campbell inherited 200 acres of the current project area and another 226 acres (now the site of the Clustered Spires Municipal Golf Course on Gas House Pike). Randolph also inherited eight slaves, cattle, sheep, hogs, horses, mules and all implements of husbandry pertaining to those plots. The wording of the will implied that Randolph, then age twenty-seven, was already established on his allotted acreage.

Edward Campbell inherited 278 acres, but no mention of slaves or other items attached to this land was contained in the will. The 1820 plat of the Richlands depicted a lime kiln and a house located on the banks of the Monocacy River on Edward Campbell's acreage. The house and agricultural buildings were constructed on the land originally devised to Edward Campbell.

Although the real estate was devised to the children, the entire property remained encumbered by William Campbell's debts. These debts apparently were not satisfied by the sale of property located outside Frederick County.

Historic Memory and Preservation

Edward and Randolph Campbell and Catherine and James Cunningham all resided in Frederick County until their deaths. Since Catherine and James inherited a house, it seems likely that both Randolph and Edward constructed houses and agricultural outbuildings on their own acreages.

In the 1825 Frederick County tax rolls, Edward Campbell was assessed for 704 acres valued at $5,632. This acreage included the property devised to Randolph Campbell, who died in 1824. In 1825, Edward Campbell's personal property was assessed at $1,366 and included thirteen slaves valued at $1,056 and other personal property valued at $310. James Cunningham was assessed for 777 acres valued at $6,216. The Cunningham's personal property was valued at $1,797, including ten slaves valued at $591, three hundred ounces of plate valued at $300 and other personal property valued at $906.[5]

In an effort to retain the landholdings in Frederick County intact and to forestall foreclosure on the property, the heirs of William Campbell petitioned the Maryland General Assembly for permission to mortgage the property. In 1825, an act of the assembly allowed the chancellor of Maryland to appoint a trustee with power to mortgage the Campbell real estate to pay the debts of the late William Campbell. The heirs argued that the real estate was worth more than the debts; but if the property was sold quickly to satisfy debts, it would be sold at considerable loss. John Donaldson of Baltimore was appointed trustee in 1827 to arrange mortgages on the property.

Between 1824 and 1836, William Campbell's children died. Randolph died in Allegheny County in 1824 at age thirty. Edward (age thirty-four) fell in the Monocacy River and died at his residence two weeks later in 1834.[6] James Cunningham died in December 1835, and Catherine died in January 1836.[7] Though Edward and Randolph were both married for short periods of time, neither left heirs.[8]

Edward Campbell's inventory taken on May 24, 1834, was valued at $5,300. The inventory provided an archive of a working farm from the second quarter of the nineteenth century. The inventory recorded 333 acres under cultivation, including five fields of wheat, one field of rye, two lots of oats, one lot of potatoes and two cornfields. The livestock listed in the inventory included 10 cows, 15 steers and 7 other cattle; 10 mares, 2 stallions, and 116 other horses; 140 sheep and 35 lambs; 15 sows, 1 boar, and 70 pigs; and, 1 lot of poultry. Agricultural tools recorded in the inventory included two- and three-horse ploughs, shovels, cultivators, scythes with cradles and horse harrows. Processing equipment included a cider mill and press, corn sheller and pieces of a threshing machine. In addition, the inventory recorded blacksmith tools, smoked meats, dairy accoutrements, two sets of household furnishings, two separate kitchens and ice in an icehouse.[9]

In the 1835 Frederick County tax assessment, James and Catherine Cunningham were assessed the value of the entire 1,481-acre property. The inventory of James Cunningham suggests that the farms of Edward and Randolph were rented to tenants during the late 1830s.[10] After the death of Catherine in 1836, the heirs to the property were her five children. By 1840, her two oldest sons were the only children older than the age of twenty-one. Two teenage sons lived with their married sister, Rebecca, in Virginia.

In 1840, mortgage holders filed a petition in the Chancery Court of the State of Maryland for the repayment of the money owed to them.[11] On June 29, 1841, the Chancery Court ordered the public sale of William Campbell's Richlands for payment of debts.

Between 1841 and 1844, portions of the Richlands were sold at public sale. The initial advertisement offered fourteen hundred acres divided into three farms of different sizes for sale. On June 6, 1842, John J. Donaldson, trustee, sold two hundred acres of land to Nimrod Owings at public auction.[12] When the deed was recorded in December 1843, Owings owned three hundred acres of the Richlands. The deed referenced buildings and improvements, not just the land, as originally advertised.[13]

On February 21, 1845, Owings sold the three hundred acres to John Noonan.[14] On February 24, 1845, John Noonan applied for a fire insurance policy through the Frederick Mutual Insurance Company. Noonan requested insurance for the following buildings:

> *Two-story, log house, 49 ft 5 in front by 17 ft 11 in deep*
> *One-story old log building, 26 ft by 17 ft*
> *Bake oven*
> *Log smokehouse, 11 ft by 11 ft*
> *Frame barn, 50 ft 4 in long and 43 ft deep with stable and sheds attached*
> *Frame corncrib, 36 ft long by 10 ft 6 in*
> *Log cow stable, 25 ft 9 in and 18 ft deep with sheds.*[15]

The census of 1850 provided information about John Noonan and his farm. Born in Ireland, Noonan was fifty-five when he purchased the property. He lived with his wife Catherine, age forty-eight, and four sons: Joseph J., Edward, Robert and Francis, ages thirteen, eleven, nine and seven, respectively. Noonan's real estate, comprising 327 improved acres and 25 unimproved acres, was valued at $23,000. He owned six slaves—three males (ages thirty-eight, eleven and nine), and three females (ages thirty-five, fifteen and six). Three slaves were recorded as black and three as mulatto. He owned six horses, eight milk cows, seven other cattle and sixty swine, valued at $2,000. He raised 1,000 bushels of wheat, 60 bushels rye, 1,500 bushels Indian corn, 200 bushels oats and 200 bushels potatoes. Farm production also included 550 pounds of butter, 43 tons of hay, and 16 bushels of clover seed.[16]

Noonan owned one of the largest farms in the New Market enumeration district.[17] In 1850, there were 2,007 farms located in Frederick County. The New Market district contained 266 farms with the highest number of acres in production. The cash value of these farms in the New Market district ranked sixth in the county. The majority of farmers (n=212) in the district farmed fewer than 200 improved acres. Of this total, 52 percent (111) farmed fewer than 100 improved acres; 35 (13 percent) farmers farmed between 200 and 299 improved acres. Only 11 farms had between 300 and 399 improved acres, and still fewer held over 400 improved acres.[18]

Noonan's farm, valued at $23,000, was the highest valued farm in the New Market district. In the district, 75 percent (199) of farms were valued under $5,000. Of those, 103 farms were valued under $2,000, while the remainder (96) were valued between $2,000 and $4,999. A total of 51 farms (19 percent) were valued between $5,000 and $9,999, and just 13 (5 percent) were valued between $10,000 and $15,999. The three farmers in the district with the greatest farm values were Henry Leighter ($19,000), Joseph Schell ($20,000) and John Noonan ($23,000).[19] All three farms originally were part of William Campbell's landholdings.

According to the 1850 agricultural census, the two most prevalent crops were wheat (740,555 bushels) and Indian corn (784,868 bushels). The New Market district ranked eighth in Frederick County in the production of wheat, accounting for 6.25 percent (46,340 bushels) of the county's output. The district ranked fifth in the production of Indian corn, producing approximately 10 percent (78,855 bushels) of the county's output. The New Market district ranked first in the county in terms of tobacco production, producing over 53 percent (94,370 pounds) of the county's total output. However, tobacco was not part of Noonan's crops.

The New Market district contained the third highest number of milk cows (1,037 or 10.8 percent of the county's total milk cows); the third highest number of sheep (1,675 or 13.3 percent of the county's total); and third highest number of swine (4,918 or 12.4 percent of the county's total).[20] In 1860, Frederick County led the state of Maryland in production of wheat, corn, rye and butter, and in the number of milk cows.[21]

Mid-Maryland: A Crossroads of History

Throughout his ownership, Noonan continuously improved the property. In 1850, Noonan updated his fire insurance policy to reflect these new improvements. New outbuildings added to the farmstead included a log servants' house, log smokehouse, carriage house, barns and shed, and wagon shed/corncrib.[22]

In 1854, Noonan constructed a new Sweitzer barn.[23] A survey of the new barn recorded:

> *size 46 by 85 feet, base built of stone, balance frame and weatherboarded, four dormer windows, cupola in center of roof, three lightning rods, cypress roof. Frame shed attached at the northeast corner of barn 24 by 29 feet. This shed is intended for the horse power that drives the threshing machine. Granary attached at the northwest corner of the barn 12 ½ by 26 ½ feet, double lined, with cellar under the same. Attached at southwest corner of barn stone cow shed, 12 by 50 feet, oak roof.*

The last survey of improvements on Noonan's farm occurred in 1859. By this time, Noonan had added a hay house (18 by 50 feet), frame wagon shed and corncribs (32 ½ by 45 feet), stone and frame hog and cow house (11 by 36 feet), frame shed (12 by 50 feet), chicken house (14 by 18 feet), and frame carriage house (16 by 20 feet).[24]

In 1860, Catherine Noonan, executor of the last will of John Noonan, in accordance with her husband's will and a decree of the Orphan's Court issued on January 18, 1860, advertised the farm for sale. The notice of the public sale described the farm with 352 acres of first quality limestone land with 40 heavily timbered acres. Improvements were described as follows:

> *a two-story Dwelling fifty feet front, with a Back Building of sixty feet; a Barn built in 1854, 85 x 46 feet, with a double Threshing Floor, and a Threshing Machine Shed and Granary, under a continuation of the roof, which is covered with Cypress shingles, Stalls in the Basement for 18 Horses and 16 Cows; with 2 Feeding Rooms. A young Apple Orchard in full bearing, and two Tenant Houses, Quarter for Servants, Carriage House, two Corn Cribs, which will contain 1000 barrels, Hay Barrack, Spring and Ice Houses, Blacksmith Shop, Smoke House, two Cow Sheds, fifty feet each; and a Draw Lime Kiln.*[25]

The public sale of real property that occurred on March 6, 1860, included sixteen horses, eleven milk cows, ten cattle, fifty pigs, thirty Cotswold sheep, wheat drills, thresher and shaker, blacksmith's tools, 90 acres of wheat, five hundred bushels of corn, five slaves, and many farm implements and tools.[26]

The Campbell Farmstead was a well-appointed agricultural complex constructed during the mid-nineteenth century. The heart of the farm was the multi-purpose bank barn in the farmyard. This efficient barn contained a variety of farm functions under one roof. The upper level was used for grain processing and storage. The lower level housed livestock. Many features of the Sweitzer barn described in the 1854 fire insurance policy remained intact until this study. The overall dimensions, interior configuration, granary and construction materials were the same. Features that no longer remained on the bank barn were the dormers, the cupola and the threshing machine shed.

The lower level of the barn was constructed of stone measuring two feet thick. The stone walls supported two large summer beams and the timber framing of the upper level. The projecting forebay, a distinguishing characteristic of the bank barn, was supported by large hewn timbers keyed into the north wall and stone wing walls. The forebay beams were cantilevered approximately six feet over the stone wall of the stable level. Large double doors were centered on the forebay wall. When open, these doors allowed a cross wind to assist in the winnowing stage of wheat threshing.

The framing system of the upper level of the barn was two-tiered. The heaviest framing timbers were used in the five principal interior and gable-end bents. The outer walls were tied to the main bents by lighter horizontal framing members. The framing members were hand hewn and joined with mortise-and-tenon joints. Each principal bent was composed of three vertical posts. Large, horizontal cross beams were mortised into the vertical posts. The end posts supported a roof plate. The bent was completed by a continuous tie beam that spanned the bent and was mortised over the roof plate. The bents on either side of the threshing floor were further strengthened by mortised and tenoned beams tying these bents to the middle bent.

The roof framing system was supported by canted queen posts that extended from the tie beams to the roof purlins. The queen posts were reinforced with angled struts. The hand-hewn rafters were pegged at the ridge using a tongue-and-fork joint.

Two scholars have documented bank barns. In 1941, Charles H. Dornbusch documented various barn types according to county. In 1956, Dornbusch's extensive research entitled *Pennsylvania German Barns* was published by the Pennsylvania German Folklore Society.[27] In 1992, Robert Ensminger published *The Pennsylvania Barn*. Ensminger's work focused on revising Dornbusch's earlier classification system into three general categories with sub-categories.[28]

Mid-Maryland: A Crossroads of History

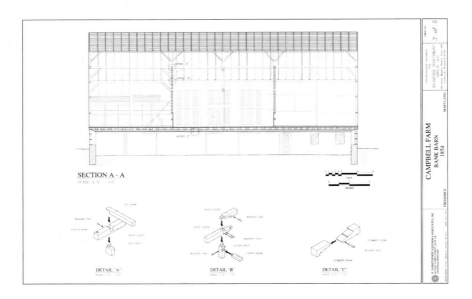

Elevation plan for the Campbell Farm bank barn. *Drawing by Brian Cleven, Justin Edgington and Barry Warthen. Courtesy of R. Christopher Goodwin & Associates, Inc.*

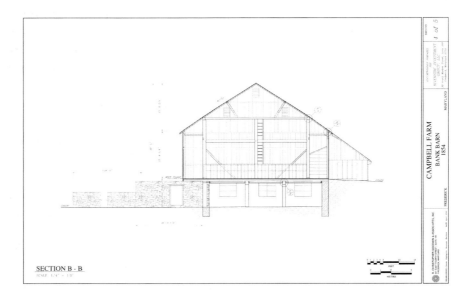

Side elevation plan for Campbell Farm bank barn. *Drawing by Brian Cleven, Justin Edgington and Barry Warthen. Courtesy of R. Christopher Goodwin & Associates, Inc.*

Historic Memory and Preservation

Both Dornbusch and Ensminger defined the essential form of the Pennsylvania bank barn as a two-level, rectangular, gabled barn situated along a natural slope or an artificial incline. The upper level was accessed by the ramp. The partially bermed lower level contained livestock stables. Typically, the central bay served as the threshing floor and equipment storage, while hay was stored in the mows. The defining feature of the bank barn was the cantilevered bay that typically projected about six feet over the lower stable area.[29] Using the classification development by Ensminger, the 1854 barn constructed by John Noonan was an example of the extended standard Pennsylvania barn type with enclosed forebay and rear outsheds.[30]

The bank barn was the most dominant barn type constructed in Frederick County during the nineteenth and early twentieth centuries. A review of the Frederick County historic site files housed in the Frederick County Planning Department for the planning zones of Buckeystown, Jefferson, Frederick, New Market, Libertytown and Middletown Valley identified a sample of eighty-three bank barns. Based on exterior photographs, the most prevalent barn type in this sample was the standard Pennsylvania barn. In many cases, the photographic documentation consisted of a single view of the barn, typically either the forebay or the ramped elevation. The inventory data also illustrated the difficulties in dating barns. In the sample of eighty-three barns examined in the Frederick County historic site files, only twenty-three barns were dated based on direct physical evidence (i.e., dates found on the buildings) or archival sources (deeds, informant interviews and secondary sources). The remaining barns were dated based on exterior visual appearance or types of construction materials.

Three variants of the Pennsylvania barn as classified by Ensminger were documented in the sample of eighty-three barns drawn from the Frederick County historic site files: the Sweitzer barn, the standard Pennsylvania barn, and the extended Pennsylvania barn.[31] The Sweitzer barn was introduced into the southeastern Pennsylvania region when the original German settlers arrived. This barn type was distinguished by its cantilevered forebay that resulted in a pronounced profile where the forebay roof slope is longer than the rear roof slope. Six examples of Sweitzer barns were identified in the barn sample undertaken for this project: F-1-179, F-3-71, F-3-82, F-3-132, F-7-59 and F-8-45. All of these documented barns were dated before 1850. The barns were constructed of brick or stone on three elevations. In most cases, the cantilevered forebays were supported by stone end walls, placing them in Ensminger's classification of transition Sweitzer barns.[32] Only one Sweitzer barn was documented as featuring a stone granary outshed.

Mid-Maryland: A Crossroads of History

Of the eighty-three barns sampled, seventy-two (87 percent) represented the standard Pennsylvania barn. These barns are characterized by their timber framing set on stone foundations and feature a symmetrical roofline. This roofline is achieved by employing symmetrical interior bents that incorporate the forebay within the main framing system. The forebay can be either open (without supports) or closed (with stone walls for additional forebay support). The Frederick County historic site files included twenty-three barns with closed forebays and twenty-one barns with open forebays; the remaining documented barns could not be classified. The dates of construction ranged from 1800 through 1920.

The extended Pennsylvania barn was represented by the least number of barns. The defining feature of this barn type is a profile where the gabled-roof slope over the rear ramped elevation is longer than the roof over the forebay. Two examples of the extended Pennsylvania barn type were documented in photographs. An accurate number of this barn type in the county is unknown since inventory photographs that depicted forebays often do not show ramped elevations. It was not possible to ascertain if outsheds were located on the ramped elevations of many barns.

The Pennsylvania bank barn was an efficient barn type. It housed grain production and storage and livestock under one roof. What caused the demise of these barns were trends toward specialized farming, technological changes and governmental regulations. In Frederick County, farmers increased dairy operations. Between 1900 and 1930, the number of milk cows greatly increased. In 1900, milk cows numbered 21,401 (21.7 percent of livestock) in Frederick County. By 1920, milk cows numbered 31,157, accounting for 34.2 percent of livestock.[33] The primary market for dairy output was Washington, D.C.

Sanitation regulations introduced during the early twentieth century established new regulations for milk production, storage and processing. Separation of milk cows from other farm animals was recommended. At the Campbell Farmstead, a separate horse barn was constructed, as well as a new rusticated, concrete-block dairy. Improvements made to the lower level of the bank barn included converting the west end into a milking parlor and installing metal tubing between stalls and tongue-and-groove ceiling in efforts to control cleanliness. By the 1930s, these changes were inadequate. The older bank barn was supplanted by the modern concrete-block dairy barn and milk house.

The recordation of the Campbell Farmstead outbuildings provided the opportunity to analyze the 1854 barn within the larger historic context of nineteenth century Frederick County barn design and construction. The analysis illustrated the continuing influence of prototypes common in southern Pennsylvania that frequently are associated with German cultural areas. The study further suggests that, by the mid-nineteenth century, these prototypes were adopted outside the German community as specialized buildings suitable for diversified agriculture.

Bibliography

Dornbusch, Charles. *Pennsylvania German Barns*. Vol. 21. Allentown: Pennsylvania German Folklore Society, 1956.

———. "Summary of Pennsylvania Barn Types." Dornbusch Collection, RG 801, SR 7.1, Box 11L. Chester County, American Institute of Architects Archives. Washington, D.C.

Eader, Edith Olivia, and Trudie Davis-Long, comps. *The Jacob Engelbrecht Death Ledger of Frederick County, Maryland, 1820–1890*. Monrovia, MD: Paw Prints, 1995.

———. *The Jacob Engelbrecht Marriage Ledger of Frederick County, Maryland, 1820–1890*. Monrovia, MD: Paw Prints, Inc., 1994.

Ensminger, Robert F. *The Pennsylvania Barn*. Baltimore: Johns Hopkins University Press, 1992.

Frederick County Inventories. Various volumes. Maryland State Archives, Annapolis.

Frederick County Land Records. Various volumes. Frederick County Courthouse, Frederick, MD.

Frederick County Wills. Register of Wills. Frederick County Courthouse, Frederick, MD.

Frederick Examiner. C. Burr Artz Public Library, Frederick, MD.

Frederick Mutual Insurance Company. Historical Records. Frederick, MD.

Mid-Maryland: A Crossroads of History

Frederick Republican Citizen. C. Burr Artz Public Library, Frederick, MD.

Hitselberger, Mary Fitzhugh, and John Philip Dern. *Bridge in Time: The Complete 1850 Census of Frederick County, Maryland.* Redwood, CA: Monocacy Book Company, 1978.

Maryland Chancery Court Records. Maryland State Archives, Annapolis.

Maryland Inventory of Historic Properties for Frederick County. Maryland Historical Trust, Crownsville, MD, and the Frederick County Planning Department, Frederick, MD.

Moore, L. Tilden, comp. *Abstracts of Marriages and Deaths and Other Articles of Interest in the Newspapers of Frederick and Montgomery Counties, Maryland from 1831 to 1840.* Bowie, MD: Heritage Books, Inc., 1991.

Quynn, William R., ed. *The Diary of Jacob Engelbrecht.* Frederick, MD: Frederick County Historical Society, 1976.

Tracey, Grace L., and John P. Dern. *Pioneers of Old Monocacy: The Early Settlement of Frederick County Maryland, 1721–1743.* Baltimore: Genealogical Publishing Co., Inc., 1987.

Wesler, Kit W., Dennis J. Pogue, Aileen Button, Gordon J. Fine, Patricia Sternheimer, and E. Glyn Furgurson. *The M/DOT Archeological Resources Survey.* Vol. 3, *The Piedmont.* Maryland Historical Trust, 1981.

Frederick's French Connection at *L'Hermitage* on the Monocacy Battlefield:

Victoire Vincendiere and French Planter Refugees from the Slave Revolt in Haiti in the 1790s

Paula Stoner Reed

Along the Monocacy River between Frederick and Washington, D.C., in Frederick County, Maryland, stands a large, stone hip-roofed barn. A French-looking barn in central Maryland where the major cultural influences were English and German seems strangely out of place.

The history of the mysterious barn was revealed during a cultural resources study prepared for Monocacy National Battlefield, upon which the barn is located. The research brought to light a fascinating story about the plantation, *L'Hermitage*, and its eighteenth and early nineteenth century occupants the Vincendieres. The barn really *is* French.

The Monocacy study offered a tantalizing glimpse of this important aspect of Maryland's cultural history. The Vincendieres were plantation owners in Saint Domingue (Haiti). Fleeing the slave revolt that began there in 1791, they escaped to Maryland probably by way of Charleston, South Carolina, in October and November of 1793. They traveled to Frederick County and established the Hermitage on land belonging to a local merchant, James

Digitally altered photograph of *L'Hermitage* with its original hipped roof and early shed-roofed addition. *Courtesy of Paula S. Reed and Associates, Inc.*

Mid-Maryland: A Crossroads of History

Marshall. Victoire Vincendiere, who was just seventeen when she arrived in Maryland, served as head of the family. In 1795, Victoire bought 457 acres adjoining the Hermitage, and in 1798 she purchased 291 acres from James Marshall, where the Hermitage had been established. Multiple housing units on the property, census records and written documents indicate that the Vincendieres, with the help of James Marshall, operated an asylum for other refugees from Saint Domingue. The buildings were constructed about 1794. Later, Victoire modified and updated the house in the 1820s. This is the only known intact French Caribbean plantation complex in Maryland.

The Hermitage lies at the northwest side of the Monocacy National Battlefield, just south of Frederick, Maryland. The French family that assembled the tract in the 1790s named the property, and throughout its history it has been known as the Hermitage. The farm borders the Urbana Pike (US Route 355), known historically as the Georgetown Road or Georgetown Pike, west of the Monocacy River and the B&O Railroad. A lane leads in a westerly direction from the Rockville Pike to the buildings, situated about a quarter mile west of the highway. The property, now containing 273.69 acres, came to the National Park Service in 1993, from the family that had owned it since 1835.

The farmstead grouping is made up of a multi-part stuccoed stone, brick and log house, the oldest intact part of which dates from the 1790s; a log and stone secondary dwelling dating from the late eighteenth century; a mid-twentieth-century dairy barn; a nineteenth-century frame wagon shed; a log smoke house; and various twentieth-century sheds and outbuildings. Set apart from this complex and to the west is a hip-roofed stone-crop barn, dating from the late eighteenth century.

Historical Background

A slave rebellion broke out in 1791 at St. Domingue, the French portion of the island that today encompasses Haiti and the Dominican Republic. St. Domingue was a major contributor to the French economy and produced a wealthy planter society on the island. In fact, "by 1789, Saint-Domingue was the world's largest producer of sugar and coffee; its plantations produced twice as much as all other French colonies combined."[1] The island, along with others in the Caribbean, formed an important link in the Atlantic Basin trade of the eighteenth century. Due to its prosperity, the island attracted many planters, merchants, craftsmen and adventurers.

To sustain the plantation economy, slave labor was essential. St. Domingue had become the world's most profitable slave colony by 1739, and in 1771, more than ten thousand Africans were brought to the island by traders. The number of new slaves had doubled by 1776. "The expansion of the French colony continued through the 1780s. In the ten years preceding the French Revolution, Saint-Domingue's booming economy was primarily responsible for tripling the volume of the French slave trade over the previous decade, and official figures show annual African imports to rival consistently the size of the colony's entire white population year after year, reaching a dizzying total of 30,000 at least as early as 1785."[2] Most slaves on the island were relatively recent arrivals and remembered and honored their African homes and traditions. The number of island-born slaves was comparatively small. The French Revolution and the resulting institution of democratic policies, including one that would have given landowning mulattoes in the French West Indies the right to vote, precipitated the rebellion in St. Domingue. Plantation owners objected to giving mulattoes such power and refused to comply with the new French law, leading to a revolt among the mulattoes, who were eventually aided by the majority population of slaves, which numbered about 450,000. A fire and atrocities at Cap François, the port city on the north coast of the island, followed. "Destitute white refugees piled into both warships and merchant craft" and set sail for the United States.[3] This first wave of refugees landed at Baltimore on June 23, 1792. Some 10,000 refugees eventually arrived in the United States as a result of the fire and destruction at Cap François.[4] The Haiti rebellion, the only successful slave revolt in history, culminated with the establishment of the Republic of Haiti in 1804.

White American citizens responded to the slave revolt by conducting an emergency boatlift to rescue the French planters. According to the July 11, 1793 *Maryland Gazette*, datelined Baltimore, July 10, "Yesterday at three o'clock arrived at Fell's Point six ships, (one a Guineaman with Negroes) four brigs and four schooners, being part of the fleet which sailed from Cape-François on the 23rd ultimo. The passengers and crews amount to 619 persons. There were, at the same time several other vessels in sight. We hear that 110 sail of the above fleet are destined to this port." While Maryland was a major destination point, refugees sought asylum up and down the Atlantic seaboard and along the Gulf Coast. Philadelphia received the greatest number of evacuees.[5] These displaced people came from the planter and merchant classes, or were mulattoes and slaves who accompanied their owners.[6]

Maryland modified its laws to accommodate the refugees through an "Act for the relief of certain Foreigners who have settled within this state, further supplementary to the ACT for NATURALIZATION; passed the 22nd of December, 1792."[7] The new act protected the real and personal property of foreigners who had not yet naturalized themselves, provided they do so before August 1 of the following year. Maryland's newspapers published the act for six weeks in English, French and German.

Some of the refugees who landed at Baltimore proceeded directly to Frederick. According to the 1790 census, Frederick was the most populous county in Maryland. It would be in this county in the fertile mid-Atlantic wheat belt that the best economic opportunities awaited the refugees.

The Vincendiere family and other refugees congregated in Frederick and at the Hermitage by 1794. Victoire Vincendiere arrived in Baltimore on October 25, 1793, on the ship *Carolina*, captained by Mr. Watson. She may have arrived separately and ahead of her brother, mother and younger sisters. The arrivals of Victoire, her mother Magnan, brother E.P.M. Vincendiere, and Magnan's cousin Payen Boisneuf were recorded in written "declarations of Negroes" brought into Maryland. Victoire's certificate reads:

> *I the underwritten Proprietor Planter of the French part of St. Domingo at this time resident of Frederick Town in Maryland State accordingly to the law of this aforesaid state of the third and twenty day of December of the year seventeen hundred and ninety two, Declare I came to Baltimore Town the fifth and twenty day of last October by the ship Carolina, Captain Watson and I have brought a Negro servant, my slave named Saint Louis about fourteen years old whom I keep for my own service as I am authorized to do by the aforesaid law. Made in Frederick Town in the Maryland State this fourth and twenty day of December of the year seventeen hundred and ninety three.*[8]

The other three declarations do not list the date of arrival or name of the ship, but say that the slaves arrived on the fifth of November 1793.[9]

The Vincendieres and those refugees who came with them probably made prior arrangements for their relocation before leaving St. Domingue. Since they left the island several months later than the initial migration after the destruction of Cap François, they may have had time to utilize contacts among their merchants to plan their relocation. Some members of the family went first to Charleston, South Carolina, from St. Domingue. Shortly after the Vincendieres arrived in Frederick, they organized a haven on the nearby plantation of James Marshall, a Scottish merchant who had developed a landholding of nearly two thousand acres along the Monocacy, most of which he acquired in the 1750s and '60s. He may have set aside a portion of his lands for the French planters, perhaps clients of his, on the western edge of his property, on a parcel he acquired in 1765, which he eventually resurveyed and named Arcadia. Key members of this refugee group were the Vincendieres, led by the seventeen-year-old Victoire.

One of the French refugees residing with the Vincendieres was Pierre Leberon, who arrived in Frederick in July of 1794, according to his slave declaration, and took up residence at the Hermitage. Born in France in 1731, Leberon had holdings in St. Domingue and apparently was there at the time of the revolt. Leberon became ill and died in January or February of 1795. He wrote his will at the Hermitage on December 23, 1794, more specifically, as he stated at the end of the will: "in the south chamber of the east wing [or building—*pavillion*] of the Hermitage estate near Fredericktown in Frederick County, State of Maryland, North America." Among his bequests was his cane, which he left to Mr. Marshall as a token of his friendship. Other bequests were made to the Vincendieres, his family in France and to Payen Boisneuf. His merchants were made executors for his property in St. Domingue.[10] This will also revealed that the Vincendieres were occupying the Hermitage prior to Victoire's purchase of it from James Marshall, and that the main house and secondary house had been constructed or were at least under construction as early as 1794.

In March of 1795, just after Leberon's death, Victoire bought 457 acres of the plantation Locust Level from Daniel Dulaney. This was her first purchase at age nineteen and it adjoined the land belonging to James Marshall where her family was residing. In April of 1798, Victoire bought 291 acres of Locust Level and Arcadia from James Marshall. This was the land upon which they had been living since 1794. According to the Frederick County tax assessment of that year, the 291 acres had "new improvements."

The 1800 U.S. census listed Victoire as head of a household with six men, twelve women and ninety slaves. In the 1810 census, she is listed with one man, six women and ninety slaves. The 1820 census shows her with six men, five women and two foreigners, not naturalized, and fifty-two slaves. These records suggest that the Vincendiere household was fluid with people coming and going. Perhaps these household members were refugees who eventually moved on to their own properties or to France or Haiti. The ninety slaves enumerated in the 1800 and 1810 censuses made Victoire one of the largest slaveholders in Frederick County, and indeed in the state of Maryland, at that time. Some or all of these slaves were imported from St. Domingue. The slaves may have actually belonged to Victoire, or to the other French refugees residing with her.

Mid-Maryland: A Crossroads of History

Apparently, though, there was concern, even alarm, in the United States about the importation of French slaves and the possibility that they would incite American slaves to revolt. According to Julius Sherrard Scott, "the influx of the French émigrés made a strong impression on the mind of North American Slaves and free blacks as they pieced together the details of the slave uprising in the Caribbean." Scott further reports that among fifteen hundred refugees arriving in Baltimore between July 10 and 22, 1793, five hundred were Negroes or mulattoes.[11] It is possible that most of the slaves listed with Victoire in 1800 and 1810 were from St. Domingue.

Among the refugees in Frederick and at the Hermitage, was Payen Boisneuf, Magnan Vincendiere's cousin, who arrived from St. Domingue at the same time as the Vincendieres. He was born in St. Domingue in 1738. His will, made August 15, 1810 (six years after Haiti had become an independent republic), asserts that one day his property on the island would be returned to him. "Although I am barred at this time from the use of my goods in Saint Domingue because of the slave revolt, which neither destroys nor alters my right of ownership, for I have no doubt the power of France will subdue the revolted slaves and soon resume possession of that island, declared an integral part of France."[12] He went on to bequeath all of his property to the "Misses Vincendiere, daughters of the late Etienne de la Vincendiere, my kinsman," and Magnan, his wife (these daughters would be Victoire, Emerentienne, Adelaide, born in 1789 and Helene born in 1794). Boisneuf was a leader in the trade system of St. Domingue, and was instrumental in arranging shipments to and from the island.[13] He also represented St. Domingue in the National Assembly of France.[14]

In 1824, General Lafayette is rumored to have visited the Hermitage to see the Vincendieres. He also visited the French part of Frederick along North Market Street. By 1825, Victoire and her younger sister Adelaide had moved from the Hermitage into Frederick, where they built a new town house. Their mother, Magnan, died in 1819. Their father Etienne, although he has a tombstone at St. Johns Catholic cemetery in Frederick, never resided in Maryland. He died in Charleston, South Carolina, in 1802.[15] Helene, born in Frederick in 1794, married and eventually moved to France. Adelaide married Bradley Lowe but was legally separated within a short time and returned to the Hermitage. Her son, Enoch Lewis Lowe, born in 1820, became governor of Maryland. Victoire, who never married, died in 1854 in Frederick. Emerentienne married John R. Corbeley and lived at the Hermitage until he died in 1827.

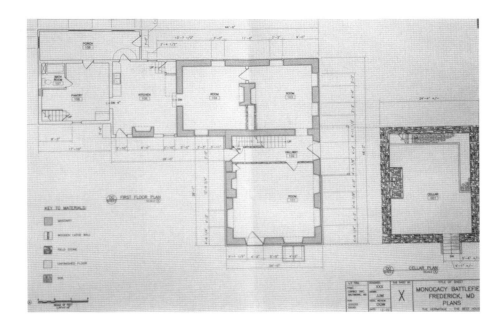

Cellar and first-floor plan of the main house. *Courtesy of GWWO Architects, Baltimore, MD.*

Buildings on the Hermitage Plantation

When the Vincendieres arrived at John Marshall's plantation, there were already buildings on the property. Marshall's mansion house was about one mile to the southeast on the other side of the Monocacy River. By December of 1794, the Vincendieres had added the "east pavilion" to the property, as well as the beginnings at least of the main house. The house was built of stone, three bays wide with a side hall, and one-room deep. The fireplaces were on the back wall. It had a hipped roof with an adjoining shed-roofed addition that was attached a few years later. A separate log one-story kitchen structure was built to the west.

About this time, the Vincendieres also built a secondary house with a Caribbean-looking second story with two living units each. The building had a front entrance in the west elevation, creating a raised door, window and door façade arrangement. Also, a stonehipped roof barn was built. Presumably, slave quarters to house the ninety slaves listed in the 1800 and 1810 census were also part of the construction activity on the property, although no above-ground record of them remains. Archaeological investigations conducted by

Mid-Maryland: A Crossroads of History

Side and back view of *L'Hermitage. Courtesy of Paula S. Reed and Associates, Inc.*

Secondary house. *Courtesy of Paula S. Reed and Associates, Inc.*

the Monocacy National Battlefield suggest that the quarters may have been located in front of the main house along the Georgetown Road.

In the 1820s, prior to selling the Hermitage, Victoire altered and enlarged the main house. The shed-roofed north addition was placed under a full gabled roof. The hipped roof was removed from the original 1794 section and it was given a gabled roof to blend with the raised north side. A brick support wall was created in the attic between the two sections. Evidence in the attic floor remains of two king posts and major rafters, which supported the former hipped roof. A brick corbel on the north surface of the north chimney just above the current attic floor level, and a shadow line of a shed roof, show the original roof configuration of the north addition. Eventually (probably in the 1860s), a framed infill section was constructed between the 1790s log out kitchen and the expanded main house, linking them together.

Conclusion

The study of the Hermitage plantation and the refugees who settled there is ongoing—there is still much information to be uncovered. Who were the French refugees living with the Vincendieres? What was the relationship between these people and James Marshall? What crops were grown at the Hermitage? What did the ninety slaves do? Census records show that approximately half were employed in agriculture; what did the others do? Were they leased to the local iron industry? Where was the slave housing and what did it look like? How and why did Victoire come to be the head of the household? The questions go on and on. Continuing research will illuminate and enrich this fascinating tale of Mid-Maryland's cultural and architectural history.

Bibliography

Childs, Francis Sergeant. *French Refugee Life in the United States, 1790–1800*. Baltimore: John Hopkins University Press, 1940.

"Declaration of Negroes." Frederick County Land Records. Liber WR 11, Folio 755. Frederick, MD.

Dugas Papers, Caroliniana Library, University of South Carolina. Columbia.

Frederick County Wills. Liber GM 3, Folio 27. Frederick, MD.

Frederick County Wills. Liber HS 2, Folio 13. Frederick, MD.

Maryland Gazette.

Scott, Julius Sherrard III. "The Common Wind: Currents of Afro-American Communication in the Era of the Haitian Revolution." PhD diss., Duke University, 1986.

The Colonel Thomas Cresap Standing Stone Project

Francis Zumbrun

Colonel Thomas Cresap (1694–1787), described as a "pathfinder, pioneer, and patriot," was one of Maryland's greatest frontiersmen, "who did as much as any single person to further the westward movement."[1] Cresap the pathfinder was a charter member of the Ohio Company. In 1753, Cresap blazed and surveyed with Indian chief Nemacolin the first road west starting from Cumberland (present-day National Road), extending sixty miles to the Monongahela River, and connecting the Potomac River and Ohio River basins. Cresap the pioneer, and his family, were the first permanent European settlers in the upper Potomac Valley (west of the South Branch), settling in the Oldtown, Maryland area sometime between 1740 and 1742. Cresap the patriot participated in four colonial wars and, in some cases, played a leading role. These included the Conojacular War (1730–1736), involving Maryland and Pennsylvania boundary disputes; the French and Indian War (1754–1763), where he served with Braddock and Washington; Lord Dunmore's War (1774); and the Revolutionary War. Surely, this great patriot deserved better than an unmarked grave. This is the story of the effort to reunite the fieldstone of Colonel Cresap with his grave.

Cresap stone. *Courtesy of the Maryland Governor's Office.*

Mid-Maryland: A Crossroads of History

In 1939, the cemetery believed to hold the remains of Maryland's great frontiersman was in very poor condition. Located on the Athey farm in Oldtown, Maryland, and part of a more than one-hundred-acre pasture, the cemetery had a fieldstone believed to be Colonel Thomas Cresap's tombstone with the inscription: "TC, died January 31, 1787." Livestock regularly walked through the cemetery and for years were allowed to graze and eliminate over the Cresap grave. The TC fieldstone was knocked down and laying on the surface of the ground.[2] The cemetery had an unkempt appearance. The Cresap Society, whose members are descendants of Colonel Thomas Cresap, was concerned about the condition of the cemetery. They made arrangements with Mr. Athey to move the TC stone to the Oldtown Methodist Church cemetery for safekeeping. In June 1939, Ross Shaw, an Oldtown resident and friend of the Cresap Society, moved the stone in a wheelbarrow to the new location, a distance of approximately one mile.[3] With the TC stone relocated, Colonel Cresap would be left in an unmarked grave in the middle of a cow pasture for the next sixty years. The unintended consequence of moving the TC stone was the risk that people would forget where Cresap was buried. Memories concerning the location of Cresap's grave faded in the collective mind of the community. Something had to be done before the burial site of this celebrated pioneer was forgotten.

To return the stone to its rightful place in the 1990s, three key challenges had to be met. First, access to or control of the property containing the gravesite had to be secured. Second, proof had to be obtained that the TC stone indeed was Colonel Thomas Cresap's grave marker. Third, the exact location of Colonel Cresap's grave had to be reestablished and verified to ensure that the fieldstone was returned to its proper place. This evidence would be found in oral tradition, documents and fieldwork.

In 1959, the Athey family sold the farm to the Moore family. The Moore family, in turn, sold the farm to the National Park Service in 1974.[4] With this last transaction, the Cresap cemetery and fort site were now public land controlled by the National Park Service. This incredible historic site was now preserved for posterity.

The year of Cresap's death is often given as 1790.[5] This date, however, is in conflict with the fieldstone alleged to be the great frontiersman's, which gives the date of death as January 31, 1787. A copy of Colonel Cresap's original will is located at the Allegany County Court House in Cumberland, Maryland. The will was probated in January 1790, which is probably the reason that 1790 is cited as the year of his death. However, three important documents have recently come to light that show that 1790 is incorrect for the year of Cresap's death.

An advertisement in the *Maryland Chronicle*, or the *Universal Advertiser*, on Wednesday, May 30, 1787, states the following: "All persons having any claims against the estate of the late Col. Thomas Cresap, are desired to bring them to the subscriber properly attested, in order for settlement. Daniel Cresap, Sen. Adm., N. branch of Patowmack, May 30, 1787."[6]

The Index of Wills found at the Washington County Court House in Hagerstown shows Thomas Cresap listed as a decedent by the year 1788. In the Index of Wills there are three lines to fill in for each decedent. The entry for two of the columns, "Date of Death" and "Date Will is Probated," by Cresap's name are blank. However, in the "Grant of Letters" column, the date of April 26, 1788, is entered. It is interesting that Margaret Cresap, Colonel Cresap's second wife, is listed as executor. This means that Margaret Cresap survived her husband and lived beyond April 26, 1788.

The 1780–1794 Book of Wills for Hampshire County, West Virginia, offers further evidence: "Inventory of the Estate of the Col. Thomas Cresap deceased taken by the subscribers appointed by Hampshire Court appraisers of the same being in such duty sworn and taken on this 30th day of April, 1787." An entire page is devoted to Colonel Cresap's belongings. Most notably, the date

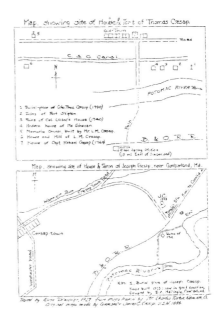

Maps showing sites of the house/fort of Thomas Cresap and the house/fort of Joseph Cresap, near Cumberland, Maryland. *Courtesy of the Cresap Society.*

Mid-Maryland: A Crossroads of History

of April 30, 1787, is within three months of the date on the TC stone.[7] The fieldstone appeared to be legitimate.

As for the location of Colonel Cresap's grave, tradition passed down through the years and documented by the Cresap Society states that the colonel was buried near the site of his home and fort in Oldtown, Maryland.[8] An 1884 Oldtown map, sketched by a Cresap descendant, shows key Cresap sites in Oldtown, including the location of Colonel Cresap's grave.[9]

On March 11, 1998, during a field inspection, Ben Cooper, Carl Robinette (both of the Allegany Soil Conservation District), and the author discovered two fieldstones at the suspected cemetery site. One was a standing fieldstone, without inscriptions, that was found buried below the surface of the ground. Robinette detected what appeared to be a small, gray rock about the size of a quarter. He noted its gray color was in contrast to the red-colored, alluvial sandstone lying about throughout the pasture and recognized it as an anomaly. Further digging around the stone revealed it to be a standing fieldstone. The second stone was a large, gray-colored sandstone stone lying flat on the surface of the ground approximately seven feet from the standing fieldstone. Between the two stones, two shallow depressions were observed, typical of what is found at older cemeteries. The two stones were found in the same location indicated on the 1884 Oldtown map showing where Colonel Thomas Cresap was buried.

A follow-up investigation was conducted at the suspected Cresap gravesite, using ground-penetrating radar and a soil augur.[10] Because of the soil type (Weikert Shaly Silt Loam) and the age of the grave (over two hundred years), the ground-penetrating radar failed to yield conclusive evidence of a grave shaft. Following the ground-penetrating radar investigation, permission was given by Dr. Stephen Potter to use a bucket augur to take a soil sample in the suspected grave shaft. Robinette, a soil scientist, took one sample between the recently discovered stones. The augur penetrated the ground approximately three and a half feet to hard shale bedrock. The soil boring gave the strongest evidence for the presence of a grave shaft. The soil material brought up from the suspected grave shaft lacked the normal soil profile compared to the soil samples taken in the undisturbed areas adjacent to the cemetery. The only observable foreign material in the auger soil sample was a Native American point, black in color and approximately the size of a quarter. The sample showed a commingling of soil that lacked structure compared to the undisturbed soil profiles. Comparative soil samples were taken outside the suspected grave shaft to compare undisturbed soil profiles with the suspected grave shaft soil sample. Samples taken outside the grave shaft had the "layer cake strata" profile typical of undisturbed soils. After examining the soil samples, Carl Robinette stated that he was 100 percent certain that the soil disturbance from the suspected grave shaft was not caused by natural means, but by human disturbance comparable to what would be found in a grave shaft.

Dr. Potter noted that the suspected gravesite is oriented east, a colonial Christian burial custom for anticipating the resurrection. Cheryl Singhal, a Cresap descendant, mentioned that the flat stone, lying approximately seven feet east of the standing fieldstone, might be a "kneeling stone." Thomas Cresap and his family were Anglican, a faith in which during colonial times it was customary to kneel when visiting a family cemetery. Dr. Potter noted that the vertical standing fieldstone was cut near the surface and broken off at ground level. The top part of the stone, the portion that may have contained inscriptions, was missing. This stone might be the headstone of Margaret Cresap, the second wife of Colonel Cresap. The 1884 Oldtown map indicates only one person buried at the site (Colonel Thomas Cresap), but his first wife, or second wife, or both, might also be buried here.

Dr. Potter observed that the knoll slopes gently toward the river. However, he also noted that the section of the knoll where the cemetery is located is graded level, as compared with the rest of the knoll. He stated that grading was obviously created by human labor and is typical for colonial cemeteries that were often located on the high point of a knoll or hill. The preponderance of evidence convinced Dr. Potter to support returning the TC stone back to its original location. He advised the Chesapeake and Ohio Canal National Historical Park of the National Park Service that it was permissible to move forward with the project.

C&O Canal National Historic Park Superintendent Doug Faris granted permission to reunite the TC stone with Colonel Cresap's grave. On April 24, 1999, after a sixty-year separation, the TC fieldstone was reunited with Colonel Cresap's grave. To re-enact history, Boy Scout Troop #10 from LaVale, Maryland, transported the TC stone in a wheelbarrow, as Ross Shaw had done in 1939, back to the gravesite. The event received front-page local newspaper coverage.[11]

On July 24, 1999, the cemetery was formally rededicated with approximately 150 people in attendance. Cresap Society members from all over the country were present to participate in and witness the event. Superintendent Faris coordinated the dedication activities, involving presentations from elected officials and dignitaries. The Boy Scouts from Troop #10 presented the colors. The presence of Cresap's Rifles, an eighteenth-century reenactment group, added to the pageantry of the event. At the conclusion of the dedication,

Mid-Maryland: A Crossroads of History

Cresap's Rifles fired several volleys over Colonel Cresap's grave.[12] This historical restoration project reclaimed the dignity and honor owed to Colonel Thomas Cresap, an American pioneer and patriot.

Bibliography

Allegany County Preservation Society. *Oldtown, Maryland*. Cumberland, MD: Heritage Press, 1972.

Allen, Irving G. *Historic Oldtown, Maryland*. Parsons, WV: McClain Printing Company, 1983.

Bailey, Kenneth P. *Thomas Cresap: Maryland Frontiersman*. Boston: The Christopher Publishing House, 1944.

Beynon, Jo. "Cresap Events Well Worth the Invitation." *Cumberland Times-News*. August 5, 1999.

Cresap, Bernarr. "The Grave Restorations." *Cresap Society Bulletin* 4, no. 7 (July 1939).

———. "Proposal to Restore Old Cresap Fort." *Cresap Society Bulletin* 4, no. 12 (September 1936).

———. "Where They Are Buried." *Cresap Society Bulletin* 4, no. 4 (April 1939).

Cresap, Daniel. "Claims Against the Estate of the Late Col. Thomas Cresap" *Maryland Chronicle* or the *Universal Advertiser*. May 30, 1787. Maryland Historical Society, Baltimore.

Cresap, Johsepth Ord, and Bernarr Cresap, eds. *History of the Cresaps*. Gallatin, TN: The Cresap Society, 1987.

"Decedent Thomas Cresap." *1788 Book of Wills*. Washington County Court House. Hagerstown, MD.

"Estate of Col. Tomas Cresap Deceased." *1780–1794 Book of Wills, Book #2*. Romney, West Virginia Court House.

Historic Memory and Preservation

Goodwin, Lt. Col. Baughn K. "Frontiersman Odyssey: The Cresaps of Maryland." *Muzzle Blasts*, August 1996, 4–9.

Kerns, Richard. "Maryland's Daniel Boone: Pioneer's Headstone Back at Gravesite." *Cumberland Times-News.* April 25, 1999.

Map of House and Fort of Thomas Cresap. Cresap Society, 1884.

National Park Service property data sent by Robert Kapsch to author, August 1999.

Wroth, Lawrence C. *The Story of Thomas Cresap: A Maryland Pioneer.* Columbus, OH: The Cresap Society, 1928.

Threatened Treasures:

Creating Endangered Lists

Mary McCarthy

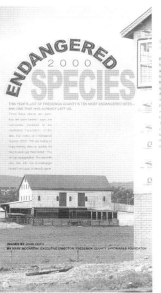

America's heritage is our greatest non-renewable resource. These [endangered list] sites are irreplaceable. Unless all of us become aware of the importance of our heritage and take action to preserve it, America's past won't have a future.
Richard Moe, President, National Trust for Historic Preservation, 1999

There is no question that with each passing year, a shocking number of historic resources vanish forever. One watchdog-way of keeping track of places in peril is the creation and maintenance of endangered lists, which have been used successfully at the local, state, national and international levels as powerful advocacy and public relations tools. There are currently more than thirty state endangered lists across the nation. In addition, there are dozens of local and regional compilations within those, and other states. Although an endangered listing does not guarantee protection or funding for sites, often it is exactly the catalyst needed to save a historic place by raising public awareness and rallying resources.

Lead page of the *Frederick Magazine* article on preserving historic structures in Frederick County, in the September 2000 issue. *Courtesy of Frederick Magazine.*

Mid-Maryland: A Crossroads of History

What are some effective ways to create and maintain an endangered list in your state, region or community? The task may seem daunting at first. Selecting criteria, collecting and evaluating nominations, and public outreach efforts are just a few of the issues that arise when initiating an endangered list. This essay will review the advantages of endangered lists and the steps necessary for establishing a list, and will describe the effort to create an endangered list in Frederick County, Maryland.

Many preservation organizations wonder what an endangered list would accomplish for their group. Why make the effort to collect this information only to then be stuck with a list of under-funded, neglected properties? An endangered list could be seen as "just one more thing" creating more work for people who are working too hard already.

The payoff for creating and promoting an endangered list comes in various forms. Of course, saving historic resources is not only the goal, but is often also the reward of an endangered list. The Union Station in Worcester, Massachusetts, was revitalized after the attention it received from an endangered listing by Historic Massachusetts, culminating in a new train and bus station with a black-tie ball to celebrate its reopening. Congressional Cemetery in Washington, D.C., received more than one million dollars in federal matching grant funds after the National Trust's listing of the site. After a long battle with developers and the McDonald's Corporation, the Los Angeles Conservancy successfully saved some of the oldest surviving McDonald's restaurants in Downey, California. This occurred largely as a result of momentum initiated by an endangered list. Countless other sites across the country might have been lost without their appearance on an endangered list.

A clear benefit of an endangered list is the media publicity that enables an organization to solicit more members or more volunteers. By putting the Pejepscot Paper Company's Great Bowdoin Mill on the lists of both Maine Preservation and the National Trust for Historic Preservation, awareness of this structure was elevated enough that within one year of the listing the mill was restored and opened as the Sea Dog Brewing Company.

Sometimes, it seems, the reason a place is endangered is that there is not enough public awareness of its plight to begin with. A front-page story in a newspaper can do wonders to reveal the hidden preservationists in a community, often serving as a catalyst for positive change on behalf of a historic site.

Endangered lists can also serve as pure advocacy. A group leaning against the sloping wall of a threatened barn or standing in front of the bulldozer about to topple an old hotel can create a compelling image and a sense of accomplishment for a preservation group. When the local community became aware that the historic 1912 Greenlee County (Arizona) Courthouse was on Arizona's Ten Most Endangered list, they rallied together and saved the courthouse in a labor of love, providing an alternative site for a new government facility in under a year. In 1996, the historic Seward Railroad Depot was listed on Alaska's Ten Most Endangered list, and within a short time the property was revitalized as the Chugach Heritage Center, an interpretive center highlighting the history, legends, arts, crafts and other accomplishments of the Chugach people of south-central Alaska.

The Historic Landmarks Foundation of Indiana, the country's largest statewide preservation group, sees the preservation advocacy role as a key factor in their endangered list, basically viewing the project as a "Ten to Save" list, and taking direct steps to save their sites. This has resulted in a very successful track record. Their newsletter has proven to be an excellent tool featuring informative articles about adaptively reused sites.

Creation of an endangered list can be a powerful educational tool. People definitely pay attention—sometimes even the people who can make a difference in saving a historic treasure. Educating the general public on the importance of protecting vulnerable resources comes in many forms, and goes a long way toward building preservation action and support. From the History Channel's one-hour special on the National Trust's endangered list to Oklahoma's Speakers Bureau highlighting endangered sites, to community groups, the educational component is a key element in building momentum for preservation action.

Endangered lists around America have been created with budgets that range from tens of thousands of dollars to zero, from dedicated full-time staffers to two-person volunteer "communities." Lists have been compiled in three months or after two years of research. These factors depend on the time and dedication of the organization, but this does not ultimately impact the effectiveness of a properly marketed list within the affected region.

While some states like Colorado employ full-time staff members dedicated to the endangered sites list, other states are able to successfully maintain a list only with a volunteer committee or even a few extra hours put in by an overworked staffer. Obviously, funding for an endangered sites list is important and helpful if it can be obtained through a community sponsor or grant, but "sweat equity" appears to be the fuel successfully running the majority of endangered lists nationwide.

Larger budgets provide for professional publicity materials, outreach programs and technical assistance. Smaller groups, unable to provide extensive intervention strategies to listed sites, create endangered lists primarily for public education and awareness.

Mid-Maryland: A Crossroads of History

The National Trust for Historic Preservation specifies that nominated properties for the National Endangered List must be "threatened by neglect, deterioration, lack of maintenance, insufficient funds, inappropriate development or insensitive public policy." Generally sites need to be eligible for listing on the National Register of Historic Places (or have substantial significance on the local level) and usually are required to have grassroots support from a state or local entity already established.

The World Monuments Fund, which releases a list of one hundred international endangered sites every year, states that criteria include the significance of the site, the urgency or immediacy of the danger and the viability and sustainability of actions or solutions proposed to address the threat.

Many statewide lists consider the geographic locations of the nominated sites (reflecting a desire to have the locations spread across the state) and the local grassroots campaigns that might be available to contribute to preservation efforts for the proposed sites. Virginia, for example, looks for "compelling" nominations, completeness of applications, diversity of resources and geography. In Indiana and many other states, geographic diversity as well as the diversity of types of buildings or places are paramount considerations in creating their lists. Most statewide lists require a listing on or eligibility for the National Register, or "overwhelming significance" of nominated properties.

One issue inevitably raised is the severity of endangerment. How "far gone" does a historic building have to be before it can be placed on an endangered list? There are several approaches to this issue providing a variety of options for groups initiating new lists. One suggestion when forming a list is to select only those that can be saved. Until the demolition of the Mapes Hotel in Nevada, the National Trust's annual press release noted, "Not one site named to this list has ever been lost." Like the National Trust, many states follow this philosophy, selecting only sites that are considered savable. For example, the Historic Landmarks Foundation of Indiana believes that each of the ten sites should be saved; they are too valuable to be replaced on the list by sites in which intervention is impossible. However, others might consider many of the places they perceive as savable "lost causes." "Never losing a site" implies that selected sites must be reasonably considered candidates for preservation "rescue."

Another strategy when compiling an endangered list is to include severely endangered sites that can be used as a "lesson" if lost. Some lists operate under the "lesson" assumption, allowing properties to be included that are very immediately threatened and could easily be lost without intervention. These "lost" places can be used as lessons of what could happen to other sites in the future "if we're not careful." Preservation Okalahoma and many others use this theory in their endangered lists, stating, "We learn just as much from our losses as we do from our victories."

Historic Massachusetts has an internal listing of "Most Endangered Historic Resources Listing Criteria," which includes historic significance, threat, community commitment, geographic distribution, variety of type and extent to which the listing will help the endangered resource.

Many groups, including the National Trust, place importance on the fact that grassroots efforts (or "community commitment") must exist before a site can be listed. In other words, if there is not some type of "friends" group or local interest that exists on behalf of an endangered site, it may be difficult for a preservation group to become directly involved in the concentrated effort that will probably be necessary to save a site.

Many preservation groups solicit input by inviting residents to submit nominations for the endangered list through a newsletter, direct mailing or website. In collecting lists of threatened sites, preservation groups often solicit endangered nominations directly by sending forms to potentially interested parties such as their regional National Trust office, state historic preservation offices, statewide nonprofit groups, local historical societies including regional historical organizations, and other local groups that may be interested in the effort.

Some statewide groups also consider larger preservation issues when creating their lists (e.g., if a certain area is endangered by urban sprawl). Maine listed "downtowns statewide" in 1996 to draw attention to the need for revitalization of these important areas.

The process of collecting nominations is also an opportunity for media coverage. A press release should be sent to the appropriate newspapers and radio and television stations letting the community know that your group is seeking nominations for your endangered list. The press release should include information about criteria for nominations, as well as the mission statement or philosophy of the organization—essentially, what the endangered list is intended to accomplish. Unless your organization has a predetermined number of sites for a yearly list, it is probably not advisable to advertise how many endangered sites there will be, since you do not yet know how many nominations you will receive.

Set a reasonable deadline for receiving nominations, perhaps two months from the time of the announcement. An effective nomination form is very helpful in gathering and evaluating sites. Information requested on the nomination form generally includes:

Mid-Maryland: A Crossroads of History

* Nominator and property owner contact information
* Property designations
* A brief history of the site
* Architectural style
* Why the site is significant
* The threat to the site
* The immediacy of the threat to the site
* Opposition (if known) to preservation of the site
* Support (if known) for preservation of the site
* Additional comments and recommendations
* Request for applicant to include any available support material such as news articles, photographs, deeds, research, etc.

Once the nominations are received, the staff (if applicable) and an endangered sites committee should schedule a (long!) meeting. Even staffed organizations often form an endangered sites committee to help in this process. Many groups include a planner, architect, archeologist or other industry professionals on this committee, but it is also an opportunity for a passionate, active group of advocacy-oriented volunteers to get involved in a worthwhile, action-filled preservation effort.

Committee members should review the nominations before the meeting. Staffed organizations like the Preservation Alliance of Virginia streamline the selection process by creating a "staff report" of nominated sites, perhaps even narrowing the field if there are incomplete or inappropriate nominations that do not meet the criteria.

At the selection meeting, nomination forms can be reviewed, discussed and sorted into categories by the immediacy of the threats to the sites listed. The group may sort by sites identified as " definite," those that are "possible," and those that are probably not appropriate for this year's list, but will be revisited in the future. Also, having a "backup" listing is a good idea—that way, if the list is about to be published and a miraculous save happens at the last minute (hooray!), another threatened site can be added to the list.

A significant issue in the selection process is deciding the number of endangered sites to be included on the list. The World Monuments Fund's endangered list includes one hundred sites from around the globe. The National Trust's list includes eleven sites annually. The National Park Service lists more than one hundred and fifty (national historic landmark) sites each year, with as many and more on their "watch" list. Statewide lists vary from five to seven sites, up to twelve or more. Groups in Indiana and Massachusetts have ten while New York has "Seven to Save." Many states, like Maine, Virginia, Connecticut and Oklahoma have roughly a dozen, while regional groups like the Cleveland Restoration Society do not have a defined number, but allows their list to fluctuate according to demand and number of nominations.

The number of sites on your list should be dictated not only by the geographic size of the designated region, but also simply by the number of nominations you receive. If a local organization receives thirty-four nominations, its list might be limited to ten in order to select a manageable number. Other factors that will come into play during the process of selecting endangered sites include property ownership and potential politics therein, the desire for geographic diversity and diversity in types of sites or structures, and the public interest in the historic resource.

An important issue to consider is whether properties are eligible to be "carried over" onto the next year's list if they are still threatened. The National Trust at one time carried over continually threatened properties from year to year (e.g., Antietam battlefield appeared for four years) until the threat to the site began to recede. Currently the National Trust only lists a site once. The National Park Service, which does not have a limit on the number of endangered sites that appear each year, carries endangered sites over from year to year until they are no longer in danger.

Statewide organizations differ on this point. Indiana and Oklahoma carry over sites until they are no longer threatened. Maine, Colorado, Kansas and other states usually list sites only once. Connecticut publishes a new list every year, although it will consider a re-listing if the threat is especially acute. Generally, even the states that publish new listings yearly are willing to consider carrying over a site especially when preservation may occur as a result of the additional listing.

One way to include a number of historic places without overburdening a site list is to use categories of historic resources or types of structures. Examples of category listings might include Maryland's one-room schoolhouses, Kent County's stone barns or statewide industrial mills. In 1999, the National Trust included "The Corner of Main and Main" to represent vital downtown districts threatened by development. The National Trust regularly utilizes this method as a way of including more historic resources on the same list.

Other examples of category listings may include neighborhoods, blocks of downtown buildings, scenic view sheds, etc., and certainly the listing of a particular historic district is a powerful way to draw attention to a threatened area.

Mid-Maryland: A Crossroads of History

"If it bleeds, it leads." This old media adage has long been the mantra of the press. Endangered lists can include "bleeding buildings." Local newspapers as well as radio and television stations will love this new controversy. They will quickly send a reporter to dig deep into the issues of why these places are threatened, who owns them and what is going to happen to them. Make this event a *big deal*. The release of your endangered list should be a media coup. Take time to carefully plan a big news conference (avoid the "deadline" time; early afternoon is usually best) and invite *everyone*—group members, fellow preservationists, public officials and, of course, all media within about a sixty-mile radius. A press release should be sent out announcing the news conference, although more formal invitations are also appropriate.

While some statewide groups announce their lists simultaneously at different sites across the state, others make this announcement at a statewide conference where a large gathering of the preservation community is guaranteed. Many states have found that National Preservation Week in May is an excellent time to release their annual list. Others do not want to detract from Preservation Week celebrations and instead announce their lists in conjunction with a special dinner, an awards banquet or other event, such as a state conference. Regardless of when you decide to release your list, be sure to emphasize the newsworthiness of the announcement.

Prepare and maintain an inclusive media list. Include large and small newspapers, television and radio stations and relevant websites. In fact, place the endangered list on your own website. If your organization does not have a website, you should establish one, since members of the media very often prefer to communicate this way. In addition, e-mailing the press release often provides a better chance of the media receiving it and responding. Releases should be hand-delivered, faxed and emailed to ensure they are not lost.

At the news conference, be sure to serve refreshments, and indicate that you are doing so on the invitations—the press love to be fed and other guests will appreciate the hospitality as well.

Have available copies of your endangered list press kit, including the complete list, brief property histories, reasons for threat, potential action plans and photographs (press generally prefer black-and-white) of each site. If possible, provide a map of your area with endangered sites indicated so the media can visit the sites. Work with each member of the press as individually as possible with regard to coverage of your story. And use your media kit for mailings to property owners, public officials and other interested parties.

If you have the funds, professionally printed materials (such as calendars and posters) are an excellent way of promoting your list. Preservation Pennsylvania devotes the entire spring issue of their eight-page quarterly newsletter to the announcement of their list. In 2000, the Frederick County Landmarks Foundation began producing a full-color Most Endangered List poster in conjunction with a local magazine, and using poster sales as a fundraiser for the endangered list project.

Holding the news conference at one of the endangered sites is a great way to allow the press to photograph your spokesperson announcing the list with a dramatic "bleeding building" in the background. Of course, obtain permission from the property owner, who should definitely be invited and ideally will attend. Be sure to mention in your press release that the news conference is being held at one of the endangered sites, and include directions.

Be prepared to deal with controversy. Inevitably at least one of the sites will be a political "hot potato," and this is probably the site that the media will use for headlines. Be prepared to answer some tough questions about properties whose owners may not be happy with their property's new status. Remember, though, that the political backlash or "heat" only generates more ink or airtime for your efforts!

Unfortunately, merely listing a property on an endangered list does not guarantee its protection. Your organization needs to plan carefully how it will provide the necessary technical assistance to property owners of the listed sites. A list of available local, state and national financial incentives, as well as reputable restoration contractors, can be mailed to property owners of endangered sites. Technical assistance for property owners varies from state to state and region to region, but is primarily based on available funding. The state of Colorado, for example, is fortunate to have a full-time staffer dedicated to technical assistance for endangered properties, but many times this important responsibility falls on overworked staffers or volunteers.

Remember, your goal is to move these places off the endangered list and onto the "saved" list. Follow-up will take time and effort, and will keep your group busy during the year before it is time to start soliciting any new nominations. It is for this reason that states like Virginia plan to publish an endangered list every other year, which allows for time to work on saving the properties.

When creating a list, consider how you will provide technical assistance, resource information, legal support, and evaluate the possibility of funding assistance. Expectations will be high that the group will become very involved in, and perceived as responsible for, these endangered places. The media and public will be very interested to see "what's happening" with your list. So, be prepared for inquiries and to share what is being done for endangered sites. For instance, Maine's statewide historic preservation program has an excellent

Mid-Maryland: A Crossroads of History

reporting tool, called the "Alumni Score Card," which is used to inform people about the status of previously listed endangered sites. In their newsletter, this group identifies "Home Runs" each year for great saves (the Maine Eye and Ear Infirmary, the circa 1891 building that now houses the Maine Medical Center offices as well as apartment units, which was listed as a "Grand Slam!"); "On Base" sites are on their way to preservation; "Warming Up" is for sites whose status is not so certain; "Still in the Dugout" contains "frustrating" sites; and, unfortunately, "Out" is for sites that have been lost. Each category lists a description of the site and current status of efforts underway. This type of reporting tool is an extremely effective (and creative) way to inform concerned citizens and the press about the status of your group's efforts.

Over the years, I have compiled a list of "do's" and "don'ts" that have helped shape my approach to saving endangered sites:

DO include a diverse compilation of geographic places in the list.

DON'T neglect historical resources that are not buildings—include scenic vistas, archaeological sites, etc., if possible.

DO include cultural diversity in your list.

DON'T release the complete endangered list to anyone before the news conference. Use the suspense to your group's advantage!

DO, however, leak an endangered site or two to the press in advance to keep them interested. Baiting them with a bit of information will encourage the press to attend the news conference and to report on the entire list when it is released.

DON'T have the organization's board or committee select the endangered list single-handedly—get input from your community! This way, area residents feel a sense of "ownership" of the list and you encourage community heritage.

DO send out official nomination forms and identify specific criteria.

DON'T forget to involve public officials in the endangered list process. Invite them to nominate a site, as well as to attend the news conference. Send a press kit to them and be sure to include the newly listed sites. This will help educate them so they are prepared if the press asks for their input.

Historic Memory and Preservation

DO keep nominations confidential! A neighbor may not want to be identified as the person who nominated the nearby property.

DON'T forget to involve other preservation and related groups; they can use their resources to help ensure success.

DO remember that the endangered list may be a great fund-raising tool for the group. Ask members for a donation (three to five dollars per site, for example) and if possible, offer financial assistance to property owners.

DON'T forget to include other endangered listings within your region as part of the effort. At the end of the press release announcing their "Seven to Save" list, the Preservation League of New York State has an "Other Sites/Other Lists" section noting other endangered listings (e.g., the National Trust for Historic Preservation, Scenic America, World Monuments Fund, National Park Service). This way, the organization does not have to include other endangered listings but can still give them the needed attention.

DO get help! The Preservation Alliance of Virginia, a staffed organization, relies on the assistance of a statewide advisory panel (including an archeologist, architectural historian and landscape architect) in compiling their list. Reach out to the community and get input in this major project.

DON'T get your hopes up too high. Sadly, some of the endangered sites will be lost regardless of the group's tremendous efforts. Use these lost places as examples. One community even kept a site on their endangered list that was demolished before the list was released to illustrate the point that sometimes these places are lost before they even make it to the list. A dramatic photo of the building mid-way through demolition added to the drama and the impact of the list.

One of the inevitable issues that arises in creating an endangered list is ownership. Who owns the endangered site, and how are they going to react to the listing? Property owner notification should be common practice in endangered list compilations; this should help ward off potential controversy. Of course, there will still be debates since some property owners are not going to be excited about their property's new distinction. Endangered sites may be selected without a property owner's permission, but handling the property

Mid-Maryland: A Crossroads of History

owners with respect is paramount to any future negotiations. Someone should be assigned to notify the property owners either by phone or in writing prior to the inclusion of their property on your site list.

The tone of the notification should be positive and emphasize the importance of the historic place (perhaps lead with something like, "Congratulations! Your historic site has been named as one of the most important places to save in our region."). In addition, keep property owners informed of developments such as the time of the press conference to release the list, any feedback from the community and so forth.

Many groups with endangered lists across the country have found that even the threat of "public shame" through an endangered listing may sometimes be enough to force a neglectful owner to "fess up" and find a new dedication to historic preservation. You may be able to save a property simply by telling a developer with a business interest in the community that his or her property is going to be on the endangered list. Obviously, if this occurs, the media will provide public exposure. You will still encounter irate property owners, but even they will appreciate advance warning of your list's release.

Politics will almost always play a part in one or more of your endangered sites. Is the mayor close friends with the owner (or perhaps he is the actual owner, himself) of a crumbling downtown commercial building? Does one of your group's major funders have a financial interest in a piece of farmland you are trying to save? Will a listing incite a notoriously "bulldoze-happy" developer to pre-empt your efforts by a midnight demolition to avoid further negative publicity?

These issues and others can create particularly sticky situations when a list is coming together. Basically, your group will need to have a cost/benefit analysis discussion about each of the sites and how politically charged a listing may become. The Historic Landmarks Foundation of Indiana includes properties regardless of their political implications, with the overall goal of saving the structure in mind. Most statewide preservation groups tend to follow this line of thinking, with the preservation of the site deemed more important than the politics that may surround the site.

Frederick County is the largest county and contains the second largest city in the state of Maryland. The Frederick County Landmarks Foundation (FCLF) is a local, all-volunteer, nonprofit organization formed "to provide leadership and to actively pursue the preservation of historic, cultural and natural sites in Frederick County, Maryland, and to increase knowledge and appreciation of these resources." Because Frederick County is one of the fastest growing counties in the state with a number of historic places having been lost to sprawl development, FCLF decided to initiate a countywide endangered list in 2000. An endangered sites committee was created to handle nominations, compile the list and maintain public relations.

The entire process took six months, from the nominations to list release, with a budget of less than five hundred dollars. FCLF sent out press releases to the two local newspapers, two local television stations, a regional magazine and four local radio stations soliciting nominations. The group also advertised the list in the local paper, ensuring that county residents would have the opportunity to participate. The press releases and ads invited residents to call for a nomination form, and mentioned that the list would be released in a few months.

About two dozen nominations were received. The endangered sites committee reviewed the applications, selected eleven sites and began notifying property owners of the listings. FCLF chose to include one structure that was "beyond saving" in order to educate the public, who would probably never have heard of the building otherwise. No one in the public or press was informed of any endangered site listing before property owners were notified.

The Maryland-based regional *Frederick Magazine* was interested in covering the story and wanted to exclusively report on the complete list. Although two or three sites were leaked to other media that wanted to report on the announcement of the list prior to its release (advance coverage included a full-page newspaper feature and half-hour television special that ran the day of the announcement), no one was able to obtain the complete endangered list before the press conference. The news conference was intentionally held on the date of the release of the magazine, a copy of which was passed out to attendees and featured full color glossy photos of the endangered sites.

The news conference, complete with wine and hors d'oeuvres, was held at one of the endangered sites, the John Derr house, an eighteenth-century stone tavern owned by a developer who granted permission for the use of the property and was invited to attend. With all the cameras and microphones on, the developer offered to donate the house and land to FCLF, creating even more media interest.

The announcement at the news conference that Frederick Memorial Hospital was planning to demolish its original, functioning 1900s hospital building (thus earning a listing as an endangered site), was received with much interest and, in fact, appeared as the leading front-page headline in the next day's paper. This generated a large number of letters to the editor questioning the hospital's decision. Nevertheless, the old building has since been demolished.

Mid-Maryland: A Crossroads of History

Hope Hill colored school, also known as Hopeland School. *Courtesy of Janet Davis, Frederick County Department of Planning and Zoning, 1991.*

Derr House. *Editors' collection.*

Historic Memory and Preservation

The other endangered places included a bridge, a train station, the historic mills in the county, several farmsteads, a downtown block and several others. Within thirty days of the news conference, two of the sites—a farm (Sheffer) that served as a Civil War hospital, and a two-room schoolhouse (Hope Hill Colored School)—were auctioned and purchased by individuals with plans for restoration. One of the county's best stone mills is now undergoing restoration in order to function as an antique shop and mill museum. The FCLF also had planned to use the eighteenth-century stone tavern John Derr house as their new headquarters.

Since the release of the list, the media has reported periodically on the status of the list and the FCLF has provided some technical assistance to the property owners, such as offering information about available tax incentive programs. Although the organization has operated on an all-volunteer basis for over twenty-five years, the board voted to hire an executive director, in part because of the overwhelming interest and community support generated by the endangered list.

The media coverage for the list launch was complete, thorough and well received by citizens and media professionals alike. The FCLF created

Beatty-Cramer House: a work in progress. *Editors' collection.*

Mid-Maryland: A Crossroads of History

a captioned poster of each site to supplement presentations to various local groups as well as a presentation at the state historic preservation conference. To promote their second list, the group will work with the local magazine to create a large color poster of all the endangered sites for sale as a fundraiser for the program.

Working in the preservation arena can be immensely satisfying, but also frustrating, and most of all challenging. The rewards of protecting significant sites is probably best summarized by Pam Sides of the Historic South Dakota Foundation:

> *Each of the twelve "Places in Peril" nominees stands on its own as a place of importance in South Dakota's heritage. Each faces a specific, at times immediate, threat. Some are jeopardized by city sprawl. Many are in the grip of neglectful owners. Still others are simply buildings deemed "negative assets." The purpose of Historic South Dakota Foundation's list isn't to point the finger of blame, but to alert the citizens of South Dakota (and others) who can make a difference. And, with that difference, we can avert the loss of these irreplaceable historic resources.*

Contributors

BRIAN BARACZ attends the University of Maryland Baltimore County and is pursuing a degree in history. He is a ranger for the National Park Service at Antietam National Battlefield in Sharpsburg, Maryland. Baracz has lectured to local Civil War Roundtables and seminars as well as to the Sons of Confederate Veterans. Baracz is originally from Cleveland, Ohio, but now lives in Frederick, Maryland, with his wife, Michelle.

JESSICA A. CANNON holds an AA degree from Frederick Community College as well as a BA degree in history from Wake Forest University. She is currently pursuing a PhD in American history at Rice University. Cannon has worked for the Catoctin Center for Regional Studies and the *Journal of Southern History*.

CHERYL FOX is a program specialist in the Manuscript Division at the Library of Congress. She is the former director of collection and exhibitions at the Reginald F. Lewis Museum of Maryland's African American History and Culture.

KATHERINE E. GRANDINE received an MA in American civilization with an emphasis on historic preservation from George Washington University in 1983. She has been professionally active in the field of historic preservation since 1981, with project experience including historic research, architectural surveys in Washington, D.C., Maryland and Virginia, Historic American Buildings Survey documentation, National Register of Historic Places nominations, local landmarks and historic district nominations, and a survey of historically

Mid-Maryland: A Crossroads of History

significant family housing for the Department of Defense. Grandine has been employed by R. Goodwin & Associates, Inc., since 1991.

DEAN HERRIN, co-founder of the Catoctin Center for Regional Studies, is the National Park Service coordinator of the center and edits the Catoctin Center's magazine, *Catoctin History*. He received a PhD in American history from the Hagley Program, University of Delaware. His research interests include a new annotated edition of James W.C. Pennington's autobiography.

MARY T. MCCARTHY has written over two hundred newspaper and magazine articles in regional and national publications, including the *Baltimore Sun*, *Philadelphia Inquirer* and *Victorian Homes* magazine. A graduate of Western Maryland College, she is the author of *Cape May for All Seasons*, featuring America's oldest seaside resort. As a historic preservation consultant, McCarthy's clients have included Scenic America, the National Trust for Historic Preservation, Frederick County Landmarks Foundation, Preservation Howard County and the Town of Centreville, Maryland.

MICHAEL A. POWELL is a professor of history and political science at Frederick Community College, where he teaches courses on the Civil War and the history of the South. A graduate of the University of North Carolina at Chapel Hill (BA), George Washington University (MA), Syracuse University (JD) and the University of Maryland (PhD), he has published in American constitutional history as well as Civil War history. He is currently completing a manuscript on Confederate constitutionalism.

PAULA STONER REED works as a professional historic preservation consultant and architectural/cultural historian. She operates a private practice based in Hagerstown, Maryland, and holds a PhD from George Washington University in American studies, a program that emphasized cultural history, American architecture and historic preservation. Her company, Paula S. Reed and Associates, Inc., has a nationwide clientele and works with research, recordation and evaluation of historic resources.

BRUCE A. THOMPSON formerly served as FCC coordinator of the Catoctin Center for Regional Studies and is currently a professor of history and the honors coordinator at Frederick Community College. Thompson graduated from Marshall University (BA, MA) and the University of Maryland (PhD). He has consulted or been affiliated with the Maryland Humanities Council,

Contributors

Maryland Historical Magazine and National History Day. Thompson specializes in twentieth-century U.S. history, with research interests in the civil rights movement, Maryland history and women's history. At present, he is preparing a manuscript on the early civil rights movement in Maryland.

Kari Elizabeth Turner holds an AA degree in general studies and a paralegal certificate from Frederick Community College. She obtained her BA in history from Mount Saint Mary's College in 2001, and is pursuing an MA in history at the University of Maryland. Her current research is focused on Maryland and an extension of the work included in this volume on civilian life in Frederick County during the Civil War. Turner is the director of education at the National Museum of Civil War Medicine in Frederick, Maryland.

Edith (Edie) Wallace will complete her MA degree in historic preservation at Goucher College with the submission of her thesis entitled, "Reclaiming Forgotten History: Preserving Rural African-American Cultural Resources in Washington County, Maryland." Employed as a research historian with the cultural resources consulting firm of Paula S. Reed and Associates, Inc., in Hagerstown, Maryland, Wallace has documented historic resources throughout the Mid-Atlantic region, as well as Massachusetts, Wyoming and Arizona.

Francis Zumbrun contributed to the "Colonel Thomas Cresap Standing Stone Project," which involved research and archaeological field work in Oldtown, Maryland, to locate the grave of Colonel Thomas Cresap (1694–1787). Zumbrum is program chair for the Living History Foundation of Allegany County (LHFAC), an organization that supported this project. The mission of LHFAC is to preserve the cultural and natural resources of eastern Allegany County, Maryland, and the surrounding region. Zumbrum received his BS in forest resource management at West Virginia University and an MS in management at Frostburg State University.

NOTES

African American History

1. *Up From the Meadow: A History of Black Americans in Frederick County, Maryland*, video documentary produced by Frederick Cablevision, 1997.
2. See Edmund Morgan, *American Slavery, American Freedom: The Ordeal of Colonial Virginia* (New York: Oxford University Press, 1975).

Fox Notes

1. Robert Farris Thompson, *Face of the Gods, Art and Alters of Africa and the African Americans* (New York: The Museum for African Art, 1993), 28.
2. Lathan A. Windley, *Runaway Slave Advertisements, 1730 to 1790: Maryland*, vol. 2 (Westport, CT: Greenwood Press, 1983). Newspapers of this period were available primarily by subscription. Papers were distributed by federal mail to distant subscribers, or locally delivered by newspaper carriers. Individual copies were widely available for public use in private libraries, inns, taverns and coffeehouses, and were often circulated among neighbors. Some slave owners went to the added expense of having flyers printed when attempting to recover an escaped slave.
3. *Maryland Gazette*, September 6, 1745.
4. Maryland Journal and Baltimore Advertise, July 13, 1719 as cited in Lathan A. Windley, comp., *Runaway Slave Advertisements: A Documntary History from the 1730s to 1790, vol. 2: Maryland* (Westport, CT: Greenwood Press, 1983), 226.
5. Observations of Governor Nicholson: Letter of Governor Nicholson to Board of Trade, Proceedings of the Council of Maryland, 1696–98, vol. 23, 488–503, Maryland State Archives, Hall of Records, Annapolis. Original spelling preserved in this and following citations from the state archives.

6. Acts of May 1695, ch. 6, "An Act Restraining the Frequent Assembleing of Negroes within this Province," Assembly Proceedings, 1694–1728, vol. 38, Maryland State Archives, Hall of Records, Annapolis.
7. *Maryland Gazette*, November 11, 1756.
8. Ira Berlin, *Many Thousands Gone: The First Two Centuries of Slavery in North America* (Cambridge, MA: Harvard University Press, 1998), 41–45.
9. Ibid.
10. Ibid.
11. Lelsey-Alicia Bernadette Delahunty, "Such as Servants Commonly Wear: The Appearance of Laboring Men and Women in the Chesapeake, as Described in the *Maryland Gazette*, 1745–1765," (master's thesis, University of Maryland at College Park, 1992), 137.
12. *Maryland Gazette*, June 17, 1746.
13. Maryland Journal and Baltimore Advertiser, September 13, 1775, as cited in Windley, *Runaway Slave Advertisements*, vol. 2, 192.
14. Elihu S. Riley, *The Ancient City: A History of Annapolis in Maryland* (Annapolis: Record Printing Office, 1887), 29.
15. Proceedings of the Council of Maryland, 1722, vol. 25, 395, Maryland State Archives, Hall of Records, Annapolis.
16. Assembly Proceedings, Upper House, July 12–25, 1726, vol. 35, 505, Maryland State Archives, Hall of Records, Annapolis.
17. Anne E. Yentsch, *A Chesapeake Family and Their Slaves: A Study in Historical Archaeology* (New York: Cambridge University Press, 1994), 310.
18. Assembly Proceedings, Upper House, April 23–June 5, 1740, vol. 40, 425, Maryland State Archives, Hall of Records, Annapolis.
19. Allan Kulikoff, *Tobacco and Slaves: The Development of Southern Cultures in the Chesapeake, 1680–1800*, (Chapel Hill: University of North Carolina Press, 1986), 329–30.
20. *Maryland Gazette*, May 21, 1752.
21. Ibid. 1752.
22. Ibid., October 4, 1759.
23. Ibid., May 24, 1759.
24. Maryland Journal and Baltimore Advertiser, May 27, 1777, as cited in Windley, *Runaway Slave Advertisements*, vol. 2, 196.
25. Maryland Journal and Baltimore Advertiser, June 23, 1778, Ibid., 208.
26. Maryland Journal and Baltimore Advertiser, September 1, 1778, Ibid., 212.
27. Maryland Journal and Baltimore Advertiser, August 24, 1779, Ibid., 230.
28. Bob Arnebeck, "Slaves at the Founding." http://www.geocities.com/bobarnebeck/slaves.html.
29. *Georgetown Chronicle*, January 19, 1795.
30. Ibid.
31. Based upon the ideals of the American and French Revolutions, Gabriel, a literate slave blacksmith from Richmond, Virginia, advocated freedom and equality. Gabriel had intended to seize the arsenal in Richmond and kidnap Governor James Monroe. Due to inclement weather, the assault was aborted and twenty of the conspirators were executed.

Notes

Herrin

1. James W.C. Pennington, *The Fugitive Blacksmith or Events in the History of James W.C. Pennington*, 3rd ed. (1850), in Arna Bontemps, *Great Slave Narratives* (Boston: Beacon Press, 1969), 216.
2. For Pennington's life, see R.J.M. Blackett, *Beating against the Barriers, Biographical Essays in Nineteenth-Century Afro-American History* (Baton Rouge: Louisiana State University Press, 1986), 1–84; Herman E. Thomas, *James W.C. Pennington, African American Churchman and Abolitionist* (New York: Garland, 1995).
3. Pennington's autobiography also has been reprinted in full in Yuval Taylor, ed., *I Was Born a Slave, An Anthology of Classic Slave Narratives, Volume Two, 1849–1866* (Chicago: Lawrence Hill, 1999), 104–158.
4. Pennington, *Fugitive*, 207; Blackett, *Beating*, 1–2; Thomas, *Pennington*, 37.
5. Blackett, *Beating*, 2; Thomas J.C. Williams, *History of Washington County, Maryland* (1906; repr., Baltimore: Clearfield Co., 1992), 561; J. Thomas Scharf, *History of Western Maryland* (1882; repr., Baltimore: Regional Publishing Co., 1968), 2:1286–87.
6. Pennington, *Fugitive*, 212–13, 257.
7. Ibid., 209, 212.
8. Gary Jacobs, "Slavery in Washington County, Maryland" (honors paper, Hood College, 1978), 48–49.
9. Williams, *Washington County*, 250.
10. Pennington, *Fugitive*, 255; for Gruber, see W.P. Strickland, *The Life of Jacob Gruber* (New York: Carlton & Porter, 1860), and John B. Boles, "Tension in a Slave Society: The Trial of the Reverend Jacob Gruber," *Southern Studies* 18 (Summer 1979): 179–97.
11. Pennington, *Fugitive* 196, 253–54.
12. Ibid., 197, 212–13.
13. Ibid., 209–11.
14. Ibid., 211.
15. Ibid.
16. Ibid., 217.
17. Ibid., 216–35; Blackett, *Beating*, 4; William Still, *The Underground Railroad* (1872; repr., New York: Arno, 1968), 691–93.
18. Blackett, *Beating*, 4–5; *Torchlight and Public Advertiser* (Hagerstown, MD), December 13, 1827, and February 5, 1829.
19. Pennington, *Fugitive*, 236–37, 246.
20. Taylor, *I Was Born a Slave*, 104; Horatio T. Strother, *The Underground Railroad in Connecticut* (Middletown, CT: Wesleyan University, 1962), 145; for Pennington's career, see sources in note 2; for influence on Twain, see Lucinda H. MacKethan, "Huck Finn and the Slave Narratives," *Southern Review* 20 (April 1984): 252–57; on the success of *Fugitive Blacksmith*, see Blackett, *Beating*, 42.
21. Pennington, *Fugitive*, 250–51; Strother, *Underground*, 145–49; John Hooker, *Some Reminiscences of a Long Life* (Hartford, CT: Belknap & Warfield, 1899), 38–41.
22. Pennington, *Fugitive*, 248; Blackett, *Beating*, 32; "An Act for the Relief of Frisby Tilghman of Washington County," chapter 67 in *Laws Made and Passed by the General Assembly of the State of Maryland* (Annapolis: William M'Neir, 1842); Still, *Underground Railroad*, 173–74.

23. Pennington, *Fugitive*, 266.
24. Ibid., 263.

Thompson Notes

1. This interpretation can be found in my doctoral dissertation "The Civil Rights Vanguard: The NAACP and the Black Community in Baltimore, 1931–1942" (University of Maryland at College Park, 1996).
2. For a description of Houston's activities in the 1930s and 1940s, see Genna Rae McNeil, *Groundwork: Charles Hamilton Houston and the Struggle for Civil Rights* (Philadelphia: University of Pennsylvania Press, 1983), 150–51, and Mark V. Tushnet, *The NAACP Legal Strategy against Segregated Education, 1925–1950* (Chapel Hill: University of North Carolina Press, 1987), 70–75.
3. Thompson, "Civil Rights Vanguard," chap. 6; W. Edward Orser, "Neither Separate Nor Equal: Foreshadowing *Brown* in Baltimore County, 1935–1937," *Maryland Historical Magazine* 92 (Spring 1997): 5–35.
4. Memorandum to Walter White and Roy Wilkens from Thurgood Marshall, November 5, 1939, NAACP Papers, I-D-89, Library of Congress, Washington, D.C.; Maryland State Board of Education, "Education of Colored Children in Maryland Counties," 1939, NAACP Papers, I-D-89.
5. "Report to the Joint Committee American Fund for Public Service, Inc., and the N.A.A.C.P." May 4, 1937, NAACP Papers I-C-198; Horace Mann Bond, "Few Teachers Ever Test the School Laws," *Baltimore Afro-American*, September 24, 1932, 20.
6. Howard D. Pindell, interview by Jenni Hess, November 18, 1999, OH 069, transcript, Oral History Collection, Frederick Community College, Frederick, MD.
7. Annapolis Public Forum Constitution, Howard D. Pindell Papers, Catoctin Center for Regional Studies, Frederick Community College, Frederick, MD.
8. Pindell interview, OH 069.
9. Howard D. Pindell, "Mixed Schools Only Hope for Real Democracy, Says Annapolis Teacher," *Baltimore Afro-American*, March 12, 1932, 19.
10. Howard D. Pindell to Thurgood Marshall, January 25, 1936, NAACP Papers, I-D-90.
11. E.W. Pruitt to Howard D. Pindell, August 19, 1936, Pindell Papers; Howard D. Pindell to E.W. Pruitt, August 21, 1936, Pindell Papers. The quotation is from Pindell interview, OH 069.
12. Thompson, "Civil Rights Vanguard," chap. 7.
13. Pindell interview, OH 069.
14. Maryland State Board of Education, "Education of Colored Children in Maryland Counties," 1939, NAACP Papers, I-D-89; Thurgood Marshall, "Equal Pay for Colored Teachers in Maryland," March 3, 1937, ibid.; Petition to the Board of Education of Frederick County, Maryland, NAACP Papers, I-C-201. These sources cited the Sixty-Ninth and Seventieth Annual Reports of the State Board of Education.
15. Thurgood Marshall to U.G. Bourne, January 4, 1938, NAACP Papers, I-C-201.
16. Ibid.

17. U.G. Bourne to Thurgood Marshall, January 3, 1938, NAACP Papers, I-C-201.
18. Ibid., January 7, 1938, and January 27, 1938.
19. Petition to the Board of Education of Frederick County, Maryland, NAACP Papers, I-C-201.
20. "Negro Teachers to Get Pay Boost," *Frederick News*, February 3, 1938; Thurgood Marshall to U.G. Bourne, February 18, 1938, NAACP Papers, I-C-201; Enolia McMillan to Thurgood Marshall, April 10, 1938, ibid.
21. Pindell interview, OH 069; "Adjustment in Negro Teachers Salaries Made," unsigned newspaper article in Pindell Papers; E.W. Pruitt to the teachers in the colored schools of Frederick County, June 9, 1938, Pindell Papers; Howard D. Pindell to members of the Board of Education, June 24, 1938, NAACP Papers, I-C-201; Summary of the Achievements of the Lincoln High School, 1937 to 1938, incl. June 20, 1938, ibid.; Teacher's contract for Howard D. Pindell, September 11, 1938, Pindell Papers.
22. "New Principal Scheduled for Lincoln School," *Frederick News*, July 8, 1938. See also Journal of Proceedings, June 8, 1938, Board of Education of Frederick County, Frederick County Public Schools, Hayward Road Complex, Frederick, MD.
23. Pindell interview, OH 069; U.G. Bourne to H.D. Pindell, June 23, 1938, Pindell Papers; "Teacher Purge in Equal Pay Fight Spreads" and "Protest Removal of H. D. Pindell," newspaper clippings in Pindell Papers.
24. The first quotation is from Thurgood Marshall Memorandum to Walter White and Charles Hamilton Houston, June 21, 1938, NAACP Papers, I-D-90. The second quotation is from "New Principal Scheduled for Lincoln School," *Frederick News*, July 8, 1938. Other sources of information are Professional Autobiographical Outline, June 25, 1938, NAACP Papers, I-C-201; Enolia P. McMillan to H.D. Pindell, February 2, 1938, Pindell Papers; H.D. Pindell to Enolia P. McMillan, March 13, 1938, Pindell Papers; *Maryland Teachers' Bulletin* (Maryland Educational Association) 1, no. 1 (May 1938), ibid.
25. Thurgood Marshall Memorandum Re: Teachers' Salary Cases in Maryland, June 23, 1938, NAACP Papers, I-D-89.
26. Ibid.
27. William "Bill" O. Lee Jr., interview with the author, August 15, 2000. The *Annual Report of the Auditors of Frederick County, Maryland*, 1940–55, at the Special Collections, University of Maryland at College Park, confirms the existence of segregated teachers in Frederick County. The audit report for 1956–61, however, has not been located.

Civil War Era Notes

1. For example, many readers are aware of the Unionist sympathies of western Virginia, western North Carolina and eastern Tennessee. But northern Alabama, as well, was a hotbed of Unionism. Likewise, various ethnic groups, particularly the Germans in Texas, suffered because of their Unionist tendencies. Less studied, but equally significant, were the pro-secessionist movements in the North, particularly the "butternut," or southern, portions of the Upper Midwest. Maryland was not unique as a "divided" state.

Mid-Maryland: A Crossroads of History

Cannon Notes

1. The town of Harpers Ferry now lies within the borders of the state of West Virginia, which was admitted as a state on June 20, 1863.
2. It should be noted that insurrection is the proper denotative description of the events of October 16–18, 1859, contrary to some historiographical sources. According to the *Oxford English Dictionary*, Second Edition Online, an insurrection is "the action of rising in arms or open resistance against established authority or governmental restraint; with pl., an instance of this, an armed rising, a revolt; an incipient or limited rebellion." Oxford defines a raid as "a military expedition on horseback; a hostile and predatory incursion, properly of mounted men."
3. National Park Service, Department of the Interior, *John Brown's Raid* (Washington, D.C.: Government Printing Office, 1990), 2.
4. Robert Penn Warren, *John Brown: The Making of a Martyr*, (Nashville, TN: J.B. Sanders & Co., 1993), 17.
5. National Park Service, *John Brown's Raid*, 3–4.
6. Ibid., 6.
7. Richard J. Hinton, *John Brown and His Men* (New York: Funk & Wagnalls Co., 1894; reprint, New York: Arno Press, Inc., 1968), 135.
8. Ibid., 24, 34.
9. Joseph C.G. Kennedy, *Population of the United States in 1860; Compiled from the Original Census Under Direction of the Secretary of the Interior* (Washington, D.C.: Government Printing Office, 1864; reprint, New York: Norman Ross Publishing Inc., 1990), 211–213; 1860 Federal Census Collection, collection no. MSA SC 4335, film M7230, Maryland State Archives, Hall of Records, Annapolis.
10. Warren, *John Brown*, 352–53, 357.
11. Ibid., 364, 370.
12. National Park Service, *John Brown's Raid*, 44–48.
13. Ibid., 49, 55–57.
14. Henry David Thoreau, *The Journals of Henry David Thoreau*, eds. Bradford Torrey and Francis H. Allen, vol. 2 (New York: Dover Publications, Inc., 1962), 1534–35.
15. Ibid., 1555.
16. Henry David Thoreau, "A Plea for Captain John Brown," in *Walden and Other Writings of Henry David Thoreau*, ed. Brooks Atkinson, The Modern Library edition (New York: Random House, 1992), 720.
17. James Redpath, *Echoes of Harper's Ferry* (Boston: Thayer and Eldridge, 1860; reprint, Westport, CT: Negro Universities Press, A Division of Greenwood Press, 1970), 69.
18. Thoreau, *Journals*, 1537.
19. Warren, *John Brown*, 375.
20. John Brown, Akron, Ohio, to [his children], ALS, May 8, 1846, Harpers Ferry Document 75, Harpers Ferry Archives, Harpers Ferry National Historic Park Library and Archives, Harpers Ferry, WV.
21. Thoreau, "Civil Disobedience." The quotations are from *Walden and Other Writings*, pages 667, 669 and 668, respectively.

22. Ibid., 669, 670, 676, 677.
23. Stephen B. Oates, *To Purge This Land With Blood: A Biography of John Brown* (New York: Harper & Row, 1970), 327.
24. Thoreau, *Journals*, 1537.
25. Thoreau, "Plea for Captain John Brown," 719.
26. William Elsey Connelley, *John Brown* (Topeka, KS: Crane & Company, 1900), 373.
27. Thoreau, *Journals*, 1535.
28. Thoreau, "A Plea for Captain John Brown," 718.
29. Ibid., 739.
30. Thoreau, *Journals*, 1536.
31. Henry David Thoreau, "The Last Days of John Brown," *The Portable Thoreau*, ed. Carl Bode (New York: Penguin Books, 1982), 682.

Powell Notes

1. For example, see Paul B. Gordon and Rita S. Gordon, *A Textbook History of Frederick County* (Frederick: Board of Education of Frederick County, Maryland, 1975), 80–81; Ibid., *Never the Like Again* (Frederick, MD: Paul and Rita Gordon, 1995), 12–14.
2. David M. Potter, *The Impending Crisis, 1848–1861* (New York: Harper & Row, 1976), 389.
3. Jacob Engelbrecht *Diary of Jacob Engelbrecht, 1858–1878*, vol. 3 (Frederick, MD: Frederick County Historical Society, n.d.), 62.
4. Arthur Bestor, "The American Civil War as a Constitutional Crisis," *American Historical Review* 69 (January 1964): 352.
5. James A. Rawley, *Secession: The Disruption of the American Republic, 1844–1861* (Malabar, FL: Krieger Publishing Co., 1990), 222–25.
6. Ibid., 225.
7. Emerson D. Fite, *The Presidential Campaign of 1860* (New York: The MacMillan Company, 1911), 118.
8. Rawley, *Secession*, 227–30.
9. Ibid., 226.
10. Jacob Engelbrecht was a tailor in Frederick who was also involved in local politics, having served as mayor of Frederick immediately following the Civil War. Barbara Fritchie, who lived on West Patrick Street, was an ardent Union supporter. As General Stonewall Jackson's men were marching through Frederick in September 1862, she allegedly flew a Union flag from a window and uttered the famous words immortalized in John Greenleaf Whittier's poem *Barbara Fritchie*, "shoot if you must this old gray head, but spare your country's flag, she said."
11. Lenette S. Taylor, "Polemics and Partisanship: The Arkansas Press in the 1860 Election," *Arkansas Historical Quarterly* 44 (Winter 1985): 314–35. Also see, David Porter, "The Southern Press and the Presidential Election of 1860," *West Virginia History* 33 (October 1971): 1–13.
12. *Frederick Herald*, November 13, 1860.
13. Ibid., July 24, 1860.

14. *Frederick Examiner*, July 18, 1860.
15. *Frederick Herald*, October 23, 1860.
16. Ibid., November 13, 1860.
17. Ibid., October 16, 1860.
18. John T. Hubbell, "The Douglas Democrats and the Election of 1860," *Mid-American* 55 (April 1973): 120.
19. Engelbrecht, *Diary*, 75; Paul and Rita Gordon, *Never the Like Again*, 13.
20. *Frederick Examiner*, July 18, 1860.
21. James M. McPherson, *Ordeal by Fire*, 3rd ed. (Boston: McGraw-Hill, 2001), 132.
22. For example, see *Frederick Herald*, August 14, 1860, and *Frederick Examiner*, November 6, 1860.
23. *Frederick Herald*, September 25, 1860.
24. *Frederick Examiner*, August 8, 1860.
25. *Frederick Herald*, June 26, 1860. Edward Evertt, a Unitarian minister and brilliant orator from Massachusetts, had served in the House of Representatives, the Senate and as an ambassador to the Court of St. James. He would also deliver the keynote address at the dedication of the military cemetery at Gettysburg in November 1863.
26. For example, see *Frederick Examiner*, July 25, 1860; *Frederick Herald*, June 26, 1860.
27. *Frederick Herald*, November 6, 1860.
28. Ibid., July 31, 1860.
29. Ibid., October 23, 1860.
30. Catherine S.T. Markell, *Diary of Catherine S.T. Markell, 1828–1900*, September 6, 1860, Frederick County Historical Society, Frederick, MD; Engelbrecht, *Diary*, vol. 3, 76, 83.
31. Engelbrecht, *Diary*, vol. 3, 78, 82–83.
32. Paul and Rita Gordon, *Never the Like Again*, 3.

Baracz Notes

1. Bradley T. Johnson, *An Address Delivered at the Dedication of the Confederate Monument at Fredericksburg, Virginia* (Baltimore: Wilson H. Mules and Company, 1891).
2. Lydia H. Davis, "Bradley T. Johnson, Brigadier-General, C.S.A." (PhD diss., Virginia Tech University, 1973).
3. Exact date unknown; he was said by Johnson to be a lad of five in 1862 at the time of the battle of Winchester.
4. Bradley T. Johnson, "A Memoir of Jane C. Johnson," *Southern Historical Society Papers* 19 (1876–1953): 33.
5. Bradley T. Johnson, *Maryland: The Confederate Military History* (Atlanta: Confederate Publishing Company, 1899), 16.
6. Ibid., 17.
7. Ibid., 22.
8. Ibid., 26.
9. Ibid., 37.
10. U.S. War Department, *The War of the Rebellion: A Compilation of the Official Records of the Union and Confederate Armies* (Washington, D.C.: U.S. Government Printing

Notes

Office, 1880–1901), 2:496. (Hereinafter referred to as OR; unless otherwise noted, all entries are from Series 1.)

11. Johnson, *Maryland*, 68.
12. Ibid., 70.
13. George Wilson Booth, *Personal Reminiscences of a Maryland Soldier in the War Between the States* (Baltimore: Fleet, McGinley and Company, 1898), 31.
14. OR, 15, 817.
15. Ibid., 782.
16. Davis, 20.
17. OR, 16, 666.
18. Johnson, *Maryland*, 177.
19. Douglas Southall Freeman, *Lee's Lieutenants* (New York: Charles Scribner's Sons, 1943), 139.
20. Bradley T. Johnson, "An Address on the First Maryland Campaign," *Southern Historical Society Papers* 12 (1876–1953): 504.
21. Joseph Harsh, *Taken at the Flood: Robert E. Lee and the Confederate Strategy in the Maryland Campaign of 1862* (Kent, OH: Kent State University Press, 1999), 99.
22. OR, 44, 534.
23. Ibid., 60, 216–217.
24. Johnson, *Maryland*, 177.
25. Ibid., 179.
26. *Journal of the U.S. Cavalry Association* (Leavenworth, 1889), 2 no. 4 (Jubal Early folder, Monocacy Battlefield).
27. Johnson, *Maryland*, 129.
28. Charles T. Alexander, "McCausland's Raid and the Burning of Chambersburg" (PhD diss., University of Maryland, 1988), 50.
29. Ibid., 70.
30. OR, 90, 8.
31. Johnson, "First Maryland Campaign," 535.

Wallace Notes

1. U.S. Population Census; Agriculture and Manufacturing Census; and Slave Census, 1860, Maryland Hall of Records, Annapolis.
2. Jacob Miller to Amelia Houser, August 20, 1861, Jacob Miller letters, Western Maryland Room, Washington County Free Library, Hagerstown, MD.
3. Oliver T. Reilly, *The Battlefield of Antietam* (Sharpsburg, MD, 1906), 26.
4. Ibid.
5. Elizabeth [Miller] Blackford to Amelia [Miller] Houser, February 8, 1863, Jacob Miller letters, Western Maryland Room, Washington County Free Library, Hagerstown, MD.
6. John Nelson, "Hospitals of Antietam" (lecture, Washington County Free Library, November 11, 1999).
7. Antietam Board of Survey Reports, RG 92, 8W2, Series #843, Claims Damages, Box #772; Quartermaster Claims, RG 92, 8W2, National Archives, Washington, D.C.
8. Steven R. Stotelmyer, *The Bivouacs of the Dead* (Baltimore: Toomey Press, 1992), 3.

Mid-Maryland: A Crossroads of History

9. Antietam Board of Survey Report #230, Wm. Roulette, RG 92, 8W2, Series #843, Claims Damages, Box #772, National Archives, Washington, D.C.; Samuel Mumma Board of Survey Report, copy in Francis F. Wilshin, "Historic Structures Report: Mumma 'Springhouse'" (National Park Service, 1969), 54.

10. Stotelmyer, *Bivouacs of the Dead*, 19.

11. Jacob Miller to Amelia Houser, December 7, 1862, Jacob Miller letters, Western Maryland Room, Washington County Free Library, Hagerstown, MD.

12. Extract from Special Orders No. 136, September 30, 1862, found in Antietam Board of Survey Report #398, Rev. Robert Douglas, RG 92, 8W2, Series #843, Claims Damages, Box #772, National Archives, Washington, D.C.

13. Correspondence accompanying Antietam Board of Survey Reports, RG 92, 8W2, Series #843, Claims Damages, Box #772, National Archives, Washington, D.C.

14. Quartermaster Claim M-917, Alfred Poffenberger, RG 92, 8W2, National Archives, Washington, D.C.

15. Antietam Board of Survey Report #323, Jacob Myers, RG 92, 8W2, Series #843, Claims Damages, Box #772, National Archives, Washington, D.C.

16. Quartermaster Claim G-1857, John Otto, RG 92, 8W2, National Archives, Washington, D.C.

17. Antietam Board of Survey Reports, #390, M. and A. Miller, #391, Jacob Miller. (These are the envelopes only, the claims were removed and have not been located.); Wilshin, "Historic Structures Report: Mumma" 41, 144.

18. Jacob Miller to Amelia Houser, October 1862, Jacob Miller letters, Western Maryland Room, Washington County Free Library, Hagerstown, MD.

19. Quartermaster Claim, G-1857, John Otto.

20. Jacob Miller to Amelia Houser, December 7, 1862, Jacob Miller letters, Western Maryland Room, Washington County Free Library, Hagerstown, MD.

21. Bruce Catton, *Mr. Lincoln's Army* (Garden City, NY: Doubleday & Co., Inc., 1951), 329–30.

22. John W. Burgess, *The Civil War and the Constitution 1859–1865*, vol. 2 (New York: Charles Scribner's Sons, 1901), 99.

23. John A. Marshall, *The American Bastille: A History of the Arbitrary Arrests and Imprisonment of American Citizens in the Northern and Border States, on Account of Their Political Opinions, during the Late Civil War* (Philadelphia: Thomas Hartley & Co., 1883), 163. While this work may be somewhat biased, the fact remains that Douglas was arrested without benefit of the writ of habeas corpus, and so was imprisoned for six weeks without formal charges.

24. Jacob Miller letters, September 6, 1864.

25. Ibid., December 7, 1862.

Turner Notes

1. The Antietam Campaign was undertaken by General Robert E. Lee, who hoped to shift the war to more northern grounds, to rally support for the Southern cause, and to reach and capture Washington, D.C. A major impetus for the campaign was the Southern attempt to provoke the sympathies of the border state of Maryland and to engender Maryland's support for the Confederacy. General Lee believed

Notes

that Maryland's loyalties lay mainly with Southerners and that the invasion of Maryland would awaken these Southern sympathies to action and add another state to the Confederacy. This was the setting in which Frederick found itself entwined. Although some Marylanders and Fredericktonians went south to join and fight for the Confederacy, Maryland officially remained in the Union.
2. Paul Gordon and Rita Gordon, *A Playground of the Civil War* (Frederick, MD: M&B Printing, Inc., 1994), 247.
3. Ibid.
4. T.J.C. Williams, *History of Frederick County, Maryland*, vol. 1 (Baltimore: Regional Publishing Company, 1979), 380.
5. William R. Quynn, ed., *The Diary of Jacob Engelbrecht*, vol. 3, 1858–1878 (Frederick, MD: Historical Society of Frederick County, 1976), 185.
6. Ibid., 186.
7. Ibid., 190.
8. Ibid., 185.
9. "To the Loyal Women of Frederick County," *Frederick Examiner*, March 19, 1862.
10. Ibid.
11. "Misinformed," *Frederick Examiner*, October 16, 1861.
12. Gordon and Gordon, *Playground*, 250.
13. Sister Marie Louise, *Annals of The War: Frederick Maryland*, p. 33, Civil War-Daughters of Charity Folder, Historical Society of Frederick County, Frederick, MD.
14. Williams, *History of Frederick County*, 381.
15. Quynn, *Diary of Jacob Engelbrecht*, 189.
16. Ibid., 222.

Historic Memory and Preservation Notes

1. *Frederick News-Post*, February 23, 2003.
2. Ms. McCarthy is the former executive director of the Frederick County Landmarks Foundation. Her essay is based on her observations in the field of historic preservation.

Grandine Notes

1. My thanks to Riverside Investment Group LLC for their cooperation during the research and recordation of the outbuildings and allowing the information to be disseminated to the public.
2. Frederick County Land Records (FCLR), WR7, 341, Frederick County Courthouse, Frederick, MD; Grace L. Tracey and John P. Dern, *Pioneers of Old Monocacy: The Early Settlement of Frederick County, Maryland, 1721–1743* (Baltimore: Genealogical Publishing Co., Inc., 1987), 31.
3. FCLR, WR12, 173.
4. Frederick County Wills, HS2, 506–512, Frederick County Courthouse, Frederick, MD.
5. Frederick County 1825 Real Property and Personal Property Tax Assessment Books, District 9, Frederick, MD.

6. L. Tilden Moore, comp., *Abstracts of Marriages and Deaths and Other Articles of Interest in the Newspapers of Frederick and Montgomery Counties, Maryland from 1831–1840* (Bowie, MD: Heritage Books, Inc., 1991).
7. William R. Quynn, ed., *The Diary of Jacob Engelbrecht* (Frederick, MD: Frederick County Historical Society, 1976); Edith Olivia Eader and Trudie Davies-Long, comps., *The Jacob Engelbrecht Death Ledger of Frederick Country, Maryland, 1820–1890* (Monrovia, MD: Paw Prints, 1995).
8. Eader and Davis-Long, *Engelbrecht Marriage Ledger*.
9. Frederick County Inventories G.M.E., 7:214–220, Maryland State Archives, Annapolis.
10. Ibid., 8:263ff.
11. Maryland Chancery Court Case #8171, Maryland Chancery Court Records, Maryland State Archives, Annapolis.
12. *Republican Citizen*, May 20, 1842.
13. FCLR H.S. 19:417.
14. FCLR W.B.T. 1:59.
15. Frederick Mutual Insurance Company, Policy 178, 1845, Historical Records, Frederick, MD.
16. Mary Fitzhugh Hitselberer and John Philip Dern, *Bridge in Time: The Complete 1850 Census of Frederick County, Maryland* (Redwood, CA: Monocacy Book Company, 1978).
17. Ibid.
18. Ibid.
19. Ibid., 530.
20. Ibid., 502–503.
21. Kit W. Wesler et al., *The M/DOT Archeological Resources Survey*, vol. 3, *The Piedmont* (Maryland Historical Trust, 1981).
22. Frederick Mutual Insurance Company, Policy 178, 1845, Frederick, MD.
23. Ibid., Policy 654, 1854.
24. Ibid., 1859.
25. *Frederick Examiner*, February 15, 1860.
26. Ibid., February 29, 1860.
27. Charles Dornbusch, *Pennsylvania German Barns*, vol. 21 (Allentown: Pennsylvania German Folklore Society, 1956).
28. Robert F. Ensminger, *The Pennsylvania Barn* (Baltimore: Johns Hopkins University Press, 1992), 95–101.
29. Ibid.
30. Ibid.
31. Ibid., 56.
32. Ibid., 95–101.
33. Wesler et al., *Survey*.

Reed Notes

1. Julius Sherrard Scott III, "The Common Wind: Currents of Afro-American Communication in the Era of the Haitian Revolution" (PhD diss., Duke University, 1986), 13–14.

Notes

2. Ibid.
3. Francis Sergeant Childs, *French Refugee Life in the United States, 1790–1800* (Baltimore: Johns Hopkins University Press, 1940), 15.
4. Ibid.
5. Ibid., 89.
6. Ibid., 59.
7. *Maryland Gazette*, March 28, 1793.
8. "Declaration of Negroes," Frederick County Land Records, Liber WR 11, Folio 755, Frederick County Courthouse, Frederick, MD.
9. Ibid.
10. Frederick County Wills, Liber GM 3, Folio 27, Frederick County Courthouse, Frederick, MD.
11. Scott, "Currents of Afro-American Communication," 275–76.
12. Frederick County Wills, Liber HS 2, Folio 13.
13. Childs, *French Refugee Life*, 51.
14. Marriage Contract, Pauline Vincendiere and Adrien Dugas, Dugas Papers, University of South Carolina, Caroliniana Library, Columbia.
15. Will Book 28, 323, Charleston County Courthouse, Charleston, SC.

Zumbrun Notes

1. Kenneth P. Bailey, *Thomas Cresap: Maryland Frontiersman* (Boston: The Christopher Publishing House, 1944), 168.
2. Bernarr Cresap, "Where They Are Buried," *Cresap Society Bulletin* 4, no. 4 (April 1939): 1–3.
3. Ibid., "The Grave Restorations," *Cresap Society Bulletin* 4, no. 7 (July 1939): 3.
4. National Park Service property data sheet sent to author by Robert Kapsch, August 1999.
5. Bailey, *Thomas Cresap*, 28.
6. *Maryland Chronicle* 2, no. 74 (May 30, 1787). The same notice appeared in the June 10, 1787 issue.
7. The author has not found an obituary for Colonel Thomas Cresap. Bernarr Cresap, in his *History of the Cresaps* (Gallatin, TN: The Cresap Society, 1987), records Colonel Cresap's death on p. 253 as January 31, 1787, the same date as inscribed on the TC stone.
8. Bernarr Cresap, "Proposal to Restore Old Cresap Fort," *Cresap Society Bulletin* 4, no. 12 (September 1936): 1.
9. Map showing site of house and fort of Thomas Cresap, traced by Alvan Tallmadge from maps made by
Charles Paston, ? Nebanville; original maps made by Commander James C. Cresap, U.S.N., 1884.
10. Present at the cemetery site investigation were Cheryl Singhal and Barbara Mershon (Cresap descendants), John Carder (lifelong Oldtown resident), Dr. Jim Dolittle (radar operator and interpreter with the United States Department of Agriculture, Philadelphia), Ann Lynn (wildlife and cultural resources coordinator for NRCS), Dr. Stephen Potter (archaeologist for the National Park Service, National

Mid-Maryland: A Crossroads of History

Capitol Region), Sarah T. Bridges (cultural resource specialist/archaeologist, USDA, Beltsville, MD), Sonny Sanders (National Park Service, C&O Canal NHP), Doug Stover (cultural resource specialist, National Park Service, C&O Canal NHP), Carl Robinette (soil scientist, Allegany County Soil Conservation District), Ben Cooper (conservation planner, Allegany County Soil Conservation District), Roy Brown (president of the Western Maryland Archaeology Society) and the author.

11. Richard Kerns, "Maryland's Daniel Boone: Pioneer's Headstone Back at Gravesite," *Cumberland Times-News*, April 25, 1999.

12. Jo Benyon, "Cresap Events Well Worth the Invitation," *Cumberland Times-News*, August 5, 1999.

INDEX

A

abolitionists 36, 55, 57
Adams County, PA 35
Addison, Thomas 124
Addison's Choice 124
African Americans 15, 16, 17, 18, 19, 20, 22, 25
Allegany County 146
Allegheny County 125
All Saints Episcopal Church 114
American Missionary Association 36
Anderson, Charles 21
Annapolis Public Forum 42
Anne Arundel County 19, 42, 43, 45, 47, 124
Antietam, battle of 52, 87, 95, 96, 98, 100, 102, 103, 104, 112, 113
Antietam Board of Survey 100
Antietam Campaign 112, 113, 182. *See also* Antietam, battle of
Antietam Creek 96
Arcadia (plantation) 139

B

B&O Railroad 136
Baltimore 17, 34, 40, 41, 42, 68, 72, 82, 83, 90, 92, 111, 113, 117, 125, 137, 138, 140
Baltimore Afro-American 43
Baltimore County 40
Baltimore Journal and General Advertiser 17
Baltimore Light Artillery 88
bank barn. *See* barn types
barn types
  bank barn 121, 129, 131, 132
  extended Pennsylvania barn 131, 132
  standard Pennsylvania barn 131, 132
  Sweitzer barn 128, 129, 131
Beeler, Peter 99
Bell, John 52, 70, 74, 75, 77
Biggs, Dr. Augustin 97
Blackford, Elizabeth Miller 98
Blackford's Ferry 96
Board of Survey 102
Boisneuf, Payen 138, 139, 140
Boonsboro 57, 97, 113
Bourne, Dr. U.G., Sr. 44
Bradford, Augustus 82
Breckinridge, John C. 52, 68, 74, 77, 79, 82
Brown, John 51, 55, 56, 57, 58, 59, 60, 62, 63, 68
Brown v. Board of Education 48
Bullen, John 22

C

C&O Canal. *See* Chesapeake & Ohio Canal
C&O Canal National Historical Park 149
Campbell, Edward 124, 125, 126
Campbell, Randolph 124, 125, 126
Campbell, William 124, 125, 126, 127
Campbell Farmstead 123, 124, 125, 129, 132
Caribbean 18, 21
Carroll County 13
Chambersburg, Pennsylvania 90
Chesapeake & Ohio Canal 31
Citizen. *See* Republican Citizen
City Hotel 73, 114
Clinton, Sir Henry 24
Congressional Court of Claims 102
Conojacular War 145
Cresap, Margaret 147, 149
Cresap, Thomas 122, 145, 146, 147, 148, 149, 150, 185
Cresap Society 146, 148, 149, 185
Crittenden, John J. 70
Cunningham, Catherine Campbell 124, 125, 126
Cunningham, James 125, 126
Cushoca, Eleanor 22

D

Daughters of Charity 117
Douglas, Henry Kyd 97, 104
Douglas, Rev. Robert 104
Douglas, Stephen 68, 69, 73, 74, 77
Douglass, Frederick 16
Dred Scott decision 32, 69
Dulaney, Daniel 139

E

Early, Jubal 89, 90
Ellis, Thomas H. 84
Elzey, Arnold 83, 89
Emmitsburg election district 71, 77
Engelbrecht, Jacob 68, 70, 74, 77, 113, 117
Evangelical Lutheran Church 114
Evertt, Edward 75, 77, 180

Examiner (Frederick newspaper) 71, 72, 73, 74, 75, 116
extended Pennsylvania barn. *See* barn types

F

Family Visiter (Mechanicstown newspaper) 71
First Cavalry C.S.A. 88
First Manassas 84
First Maryland C.S.A. 84, 85, 86
First Maryland U.S. 85
Frederick 39, 44, 52, 53, 58, 68, 71, 73, 75, 77, 81, 82, 83, 89, 97, 111, 112, 113, 114, 115, 116, 117, 118, 121, 122, 123, 124, 126, 135, 136, 138, 139, 140, 183
Frederick County 10, 13, 15, 16, 19, 21, 24, 32, 39, 43, 44, 45, 46, 47, 48, 52, 67, 70, 71, 73, 74, 77, 79, 82, 87, 121, 122, 123, 124, 125, 126, 127, 131, 132, 133, 135, 139, 154, 161, 164
Frederick County Board of Education 44, 45
Frederick County Colored Teachers Association 46
Frederick County Landmarks Foundation 164
Frederick Magazine 165
Frederick Presbyterian Church 114
Fremont, John C. 75
French and Indian War 145
Front Royal 85
Front Royal, battle of 52
Fugitive Slave Law 36, 68

G

General Assembly 22
General Hospital Number One (U.S.) 53, 112, 113, 115, 117
Georgetown 25
Georgetown Road 136, 143
German Reformed Church 114
Gibbs, William 43, 44
Gruber, Jacob 32

INDEX

H

Hagerstown 31, 32, 34, 147
Hampton, Wade 89
Hancock, MD 90, 102
Hanover Junction 88, 89
Harpers Ferry, VA 51, 55, 56, 57, 58, 59, 60, 61, 84, 87, 102
Harwood, Benjamin 24
Hauvers election district 77
Herald (Frederick newspaper) 71, 72, 73, 74, 75
Hermitage (plantation) 122, 135, 136, 138, 139, 140, 141, 143
Hood, Margaret Scholl 71
Houston, Charles 16, 39, 47
Houston, Sam 70
How, John 21

I

Impey, Robert 21
Ingalls, Rufus 101

J

Jackson 71, 77
Jackson, Juanita 42
Jackson, Lillie Mae 41
Jackson, Thomas 83
Jackson, Thomas "Stonewall" 82, 84, 85, 87, 97
Jackson election district 73
Johnson, Bradley Saunders 82
Johnson, Bradley Tyler 52, 81, 82, 83, 84, 85, 86, 87, 88, 89, 90, 91, 92
Johnson, Jane Saunders 82, 83, 86
Johnson, Robert 17
Johnsville election district 73

K

Kretzer, John 97

L

L'Hermitage. *See* Hermitage
Ladies Relief Association 116
Lane, Benjamin 19

Leberon, Pierre 139
Lee, Bill 47
Lee, Robert E. 58, 86, 87, 89, 97, 112, 182
Leighter, Henry 127
Lincoln, Abraham 52, 69, 71, 74, 82, 89, 103, 104, 112
Lincoln High School 16, 43, 45, 46, 47
Locust Level (plantation) 139
Lord Dunmore's War 145
Louise, Sister Marie 117
Lowe, Enoch Lewis 122, 140

M

Malvern Hill, battle of 86
Markell, Catherine 70
Maroon colonies 21
Marshall, James 136, 138, 139, 143
Marshall, John 141
Marshall, Thurgood 40, 41, 43, 44, 47
Maryland Chronicle 147
Maryland Educational Association 41
Maryland Education Association 43, 46
Maryland Gazette 17, 22, 137
Maryland General Assembly 19, 21
Maryland Historical Trust 123
Maryland Line 88, 89, 91
Maryland Union (Frederick newspaper) 71
McCausland, John 52, 90, 91
McClellan, George B. 103
McMillan, Enolia Pettigen. *See* Pettigen Enolia
Mechanicstown, MD 71
Mechanicstown election district 73, 77
Middlekauff, John C. 99
Middletown, MD 71, 73, 113, 131
Miller, Daniel 99, 100
Miller, Jacob 52, 96, 97, 98, 100, 102, 103, 104
Miller, John 22
Missouri ex rel. Gaines v. Canada 40
Monocacy, battle of 90
Monocacy National Battlefield 135, 136, 143
Monocacy River 124, 125, 135, 136, 141

Montgomery County 43, 44
Moorefield, VA 90
Moorefield, Virginia 91
Morgan College 42
Mt. Pleasant, MD 73
Mumma, Samuel 99, 102
Myers, Jacob 102

N

NAACP (National Association for the Advancement of Colored People) 16, 39, 40, 41, 42, 44, 47, 48
National Park Service 13, 136, 146, 158, 159, 163
National Pike 34
National Register of Historic Places 156
National Road 13, 95, 145
National Trust for Historic Preservation 153, 154, 155, 156, 157, 158, 159, 163
New Market district 127
Nicholson, Governor Francis 18
Noonan, Catherine 128
Noonan, John 126, 127, 128, 131
Norwood, Samuel 23
Novitiate 114, 117

O

O'Dunne, Eugene 40
Oldtown, MD 145, 146, 148
Otto, John 99, 102, 103
Owens Mill 90
Owings, Nimrod 126
Owings, Richard 18

P

Pembroke, Bazil 30
Pembroke, Jim. *See* Pennington, James William Charles
Pembroke, Nelly 30
Pembroke, Robert 31
Pembroke, Stephen 37
Pennington, James William Charles 16, 29, 30, 31, 32, 33, 34, 35, 36, 37
Pennsylvania 23, 24, 29, 32, 35

Pennsylvania Bucktails 85
Pettigen, Enolia 41, 42, 43, 45, 47
Pindell, Howard Douglas 16, 42, 43, 44, 45, 46, 47, 48
Pleasant Valley 57
Plessy v. Ferguson 40
Poffenberger, Alfred 101, 102
Point Lookout 89, 90
Point of Rocks 83
Porter, Fitz John 100
Prince George's County 18, 22, 24, 47
Pruitt, Eugene W. 45, 46, 47
Pry, Philip 99

Q

Queen Anne's County 30

R

Ransome, Jack 22
Reilly, Oliver 98
Republican Citizen (Frederick newspaper) 71
Revolutionary War 20, 23, 112, 145
Richlands 124
Rockland 30, 32, 34
Roulette, William 98, 99

S

Saint Domingue (Haiti) 136
Sandy Hook 57
Saunders, Jane Claudia. *See* Johnson, Jane Saunders
Schell, Joseph 127
Second Manassas (Bull Run) 87
Second Manassas (Bull Run), battle of 52, 86
Second Maryland C.S.A. 88
Seven Days' Campaign 86
Seward, William H. 69
Sharpsburg 37, 52, 57, 87, 95, 96, 97, 98, 99, 100, 101, 102, 103, 104, 113
Sharpsburg, battle of. *See* Antietam, battle of
Shaw, Daniel 23
Shaw, Ross 146, 149

INDEX

Sim, Joseph 124
Simpson, Jack 23
slavery 15, 16, 17, 19, 25, 30, 32, 33, 36, 52, 55, 56, 57, 59, 60, 62, 63, 67, 68, 69, 70, 76, 77, 82, 96
Slaves 19, 21, 23
Somerset County 47
South Mountain 97
South Mountain, battle of 112
Sparrow, Thomas 21
Sprigg, Thomas 19
St. Domingue (Haiti) 135, 136, 137, 138, 139, 140
standard Pennsylvania barn. *See* barn types
Stonebraker, Joseph 99
Stonewall Brigade 84, 86
Sweitzer barn. *See* barn types

T

Taney, Roger Brooke 32
Thoreau, Henry David 51, 56, 59, 60, 61, 62, 63
Threlkeld, Henry 19
Tilghman, Frisby 30, 32, 33, 34, 35, 36, 37
Tilghman, James 30
Trinity Chapel 114
Turner, Thomas 21

U

Underground Railroad 36, 37
Universal Advertiser 147
University of Maryland 43, 53
  Baltimore County 52
  Law School 40
Urbana, MD 73, 77, 136
Urner, Judge Hammond 44

V

Valley Register (Middletown newspaper) 71, 73
Vincendiere
  Adelaide 140
  E.P.M. 138
  Emerentienne 140
  Etienne 140
  Helene 140
  Magnan 138, 140
  Victoire 136, 138, 139, 140, 143
Vincendiere family 122, 135, 136, 138, 139, 140, 141, 143
Virginia Militia 83
Visitation Academy 114

W

Waggaman, Henry 22
Washington, Lewis 58
Washington County 13, 16, 29, 30, 32, 35, 37, 57, 73, 95, 96, 99, 147
Wells, Charles 18
Williams, Daniel 23
Williamsport 87
Willliams, Thomas J.C. 32
Winchester Pike (Route 11) 95
Wright, Phoebe 35
Wright, William 35

Y

Yancey, William 77